LESSONS
LEARNED

My Lifelong Journey with Polio

RICHARD HARDINE

BEAVER'S POND
PRESS

ISBN 13: 978-1-64343-778-1
Library of Congress Catalog Number: 2021906694
Printed in the United States of America
First Printing: 2021
25 24 23 22 21   5 4 3 2 1

Book design and typesetting by Dan Pitts

BEAVER'S POND
PRESS

Beaver's Pond Press
939 Seventh Street West
Saint Paul, MN 55102
(952) 829-8818
www.BeaversPondPress.com

Contact Richard Hardine at www.RichardHardine.com
for speaking engagements and interviews.

TIMELINE OF NOTABLE EVENTS CONCERNING POLIO

1789: British doctor Michael Underwood recognizes polio as a distinct illness and provides its first clinical description.

1840: Jacob Heine writes the first medical report of the disease, including how it involves the spinal cord.

1894: The United States sees its first outbreak of polio as an epidemic in Vermont, with 132 cases. Other local epidemics begin to appear in Europe and elsewhere in the United States around this time.

1908: Physicians Karl Landsteiner and Erwin Popper identify the infectious agent that causes polio as a virus.

1916: There are over twenty-seven thousand cases of polio within the United States, a large epidemic. Six thousand people die of the disease, with a third of those deaths occurring in New York City.

1921: Franklin Delano Roosevelt, recently the Democratic candidate for vice president, contracts polio at the age of thirty-nine. His condition brings awareness to the disease and people with disabilities, though he conceals how much polio affects him.

1927: Roosevelt forms the Georgia Warm Springs Foundation around thermal springs in west Georgia that provide relief and rehabilitation for polio victims.

1929: Philip Drinker, PhD, and Louis Shaw, MD, develop the "iron lung," an artificial respirator for patients suffering from paralytic polio. The machine, originally called the Drinker respirator, provides breathing support for people suffering from paralysis of the diaphragm.

1930s: Two of the three strains of the poliovirus are discovered.

1931: Scientists create the first filter to separate viruses from bacteria. Once they can do this, they are able to do research on the poliovirus.

1935: The first polio vaccines are tested, but several children who receive them become paralyzed where the treatment is given, and a few die. The backlash to these deaths ends the study and sets back vaccine development for a number of years.

1938: Roosevelt, now president, founds the National Foundation for Infantile Paralysis, which later becomes the March of Dimes.

1940: Australian nurse Sister Elizabeth Kenny travels across the US to demonstrate her new treatment for polio, using warm compresses and passive exercises to relax painful, contracting muscles and recall function in unaffected neural pathways.

1947 – 50: As polio outbreaks increase in size across the US, and parents fear letting their children go outside in the peak summer season, Dr. Jonas Salk develops a research program at the University of Pittsburgh. He grows the virus with a tissue culture method created by John Enders, Frederick Robbins, and Thomas Weller at Harvard University in 1949.

1949: Johns Hopkins University researchers David Bodian, MD, PhD, and Isabel Morgan, PhD, publish a paper identifying the three types of poliovirus. Their work is key to developing the vaccine, which would need to produce immunity to all three types. Further research by Salk confirms their findings.

1952: 57,628 polio cases are reported in the US, emphasizing the need for a vaccine.

1953: Salk and his associates develop an inactivated (dead), injected vaccine. Salk injects himself, his wife, and his three sons with his vaccine.

1954: Nearly two million children take part in vaccination trials.

1955: Dr. Thomas Francis announces the vaccine's approval on April 12, the tenth anniversary of President Roosevelt's death. The National Infantile Paralysis Foundation initially goes into debt to bring the vaccine to the public, but fundraising efforts help.

1955 – 57: The incidence of polio in the US falls by 85 to 90 percent.

1960: Albert Sabin's live poliovirus vaccine, which provides protection against Type 1 poliovirus and is given orally, is licensed by the US Surgeon General. Vaccines for Types 2 and 3 follow before a 1963 vaccine combines all three types. The Salk vaccine is replaced by the Sabin vaccine because it is easier to administer and cheaper.

1968: The Architectural Barriers Act passes. It requires that all federally financed buildings are accessible to people with disabilities.

1979: The last known case of the wild virus in the US is identified.

1980s: Post-polio syndrome, a condition that can affect polio survivors decades after their infection, is identified.

1988: Rotary International, the Pan American Health Organization, the World Health Organization, the Centers for Disease Control, and UNICEF begin an effort to end polio transmission around the world.

1990: The Americans with Disabilities Act passes, providing legal protections for people with disabilities.

1994 - 95: A survey estimates that there are about a million polio survivors in the US. Researchers estimate that post-polio syndrome affects 25 to 40 percent of survivors.

2000: The US returns to a version of the Salk vaccine due to concerns about polio developing from Sabin's oral vaccine, now that the wild virus has been eradicated in the US. Sabin's vaccine continues to be used in parts of the world where polio still circulates.

2017: Polio remains endemic in only three countries: Afghanistan, Nigeria, and Pakistan.

PREFACE:

ANTERIOR BULBAR POLIOMYELITIS

The polio epidemic of the 1940s and early '50s affected thousands of children. In 1952 alone, nearly sixty thousand American children contracted the virus, and over three thousand died. On September 30, 1951, I was diagnosed, at the age of nine months, with anterior bulbar poliomyelitis, the most severe type of polio with a 90 percent fatality rate.

Anterior bulbar poliomyelitis is a viral disease of the central nervous system that causes inflammation and damage to nerve cells and tissue in the lower brain and spinal cord. Initial symptoms are headache, fever, and stiff muscles progressing to severe tightness of the neck, back, and hamstrings. The motor nerves of the spinal cord are affected; they control muscle function. Other motor nerve cells in the body will compensate for those that are damaged.

A progressive decrease in muscle strength in the affected areas happens around fifty years of age. This is referred to as post-polio syndrome. The late effects are decreasing muscle strength, breathing and swallowing issues, speaking difficulties, muscle and joint pain, and inability to attain and enjoy restful sleep. The cause is attributed to nerve cells working overtime to compensate for nerves that were lost as a result of the poliovirus. Cold intolerance is one of the symptoms, making the air temperature seem twenty to thirty degrees colder than it actually is, causing muscle strength to drop as much as 75 percent. So much for enjoying Minnesota winters.

My journey, from birth through the use of an iron lung and numerous surgeries into adulthood taught me many lessons, which I'm now sharing.

1

EARLY YEARS

*"The two most important days in your life are the day
you are born and the day you find out why."*

—Mark Twain

On November 4, 1950, at 4:15 a.m. at Galesburg Cottage
Hospital in Galesburg, Illinois, the temperature outside
was thirty-six degrees and Ken Hardine was sitting inside the doctor's lounge with Dr. Gordon Behrents. Their
discussion focused on the winter weather and planning a
New Year's Eve party for their group of friends from Trinity Lutheran Church. They were interrupted by a knock on
the door. A nurse entered and encouraged Ken to go to the
maternity ward to join his wife, Marge. She was starting
to give birth, and he should probably be there. He put out
his cigarette and hastily went to the maternity ward. He
was with Marge as she gave birth to their new son at 4:22
a.m.—me. I was six pounds, six ounces, and my parents
named me Richard Grant Hardine. Needless to say, they

were both extremely happy they had a healthy baby boy.

With all the excitement, the usual New Year's Eve party did not happen, but my parents' friends and family came by to visit me and congratulate them. I had all of the typical newborn baby tests and trips to the doctor in between these visits. My older sister Kendra was excited to have a baby brother, even though the attention she got from Mom and Dad would have to be shared.

At nine months of age, I woke up with a cough and temperature. My mother, an experienced registered nurse, sensed something was wrong, so off to the doctor we went. Dr. Behrents discussed the possibility that I could have polio and recommended I be taken by ambulance to Saint Francis Medical Center in Peoria, Illinois. I was given two blood transfusions and experimental new drugs, convalescent serum and staphylococcus aureo, both used as polio treatments. While there, my parents noticed my illness had worsened; only my head and neck would move. Anterior bulbar poliomyelitis was diagnosed. This was the start of my lifelong journey with polio.

I've never known how I got the virus, but it was thought that ingesting unclean water or contact with another carrier was to blame. My early years after the diagnosis were spent in the hospital, where I had numerous blood transfusions and casting on both of my legs to keep each leg straight and prevent the muscles from becoming fixed in a permanent position, referred to as contractures. Being totally paralyzed and unable to breathe on my own, I was placed in an iron lung that would provide alternate pressure for breathing twenty-four hours a day, for many months. This large piece of medical equipment looked like a fifty-five-gallon drum with a porthole for my head to stick out of and portholes on both sides of my body, so the nursing staff would be able to give daily care and range-of-motion exercises. My first clear memory after that would come about three years later in an operating room at Chicago Wesley Memorial Hospital.

In March 1952, at the age of fifteen months, I was able to use my arms to move on a limited basis. Two months later, my doctor in Peoria ordered custom bilateral leg braces for me. I had the pleasure of wearing those every day for eighteen months until Mom and I made a trip to Chicago, one hundred fifty miles northeast from our home, for an evaluation and discussion of a treatment plan with Dr. Robert T. McElvenny. Mom had spent considerable time making contacts to locate the best doctors. Dr. McElvenny had been recommended to Mom by Dr. Michael DeBakey, whom she had worked for as a scrub nurse out of college. Dr. DeBakey also recommended another pediatric surgeon in Shreveport, Louisiana, Dr. Gene Caldwell. With the diagnosis of anterior bulbar poliomyelitis, they were aware of possible dire outcomes. Both Dr. McElvenny and Dr. Caldwell were known for their knowledge and expertise in orthopedic surgery and treatment of pediatric polio victims.

They planned a new procedure called bilateral hamstring transplant for the future. The hamstring muscles from the back of each of my legs would be relocated from the insertion point below my knees to a new insertion point over the top of my knees. This would allow for knee extension and limited movement. My quadriceps muscles on each leg had atrophied from the eighteen months I was paralyzed and, consequently, were non-functioning (the same was true for my abdominal and chest muscles), so this procedure was necessary.

Before the transplant surgery could happen, doctors decided to apply full leg casts (called wedging casts) to both legs to maintain a full knee extension position. I was then discharged from the hospital after a couple weeks to go home and be as active as possible and enjoy my friends. Six months later, I took another trip to Wesley Memorial Hospital, so doctors could remove the existing casts on both legs, evaluate the extension of my knees, and apply new casts to keep my leg extension as straight as possible.

The ride home was on a Burlington Northern train, the Denver Zephyr. I was so excited to be on a train I forgot I had casts on both legs. I spent most of the time in the Vista Dome car, basically a train car with a set of dome windows on a second level so you could see for miles in all directions. This would be our mode of transportation in the coming years. I always wanted to go back to Chicago because the dome car was fun.

2

SURGERIES BEGIN

"Don't handicap your children
by making their life easy."
—Robert Heinlein

By August 1953, being home was truly a joy, even with both of my legs in casts. My parents made it very clear from the start that I was to be as mobile as I possibly could by using my own strength. Their friends frowned upon this. They thought my parents should do things for me, like getting me toys from across the room.

My parents did assist in getting me upstairs to my bedroom on the second floor when it was time to nap or sleep. I quickly learned that if I wanted to be with people or play with toys downstairs, I would have to figure out a way to get to the first floor. This didn't take too long once I discovered crying for Mom would not work. I would get off the bed onto the floor and push myself forward with my arms while using my casts as runners. This was particularly exciting when I slid down the steps, like somebody would do in a sled down a snow hill, but a lot bumpier. Mom, however, was not real happy about the white skid marks that the plaster casts left on the carpet from the bedroom, down the stairs, to the front room. I had numerous tumbles on the stairs—no injuries, just Mom running to see what had happened. She quit wondering if I was all right after about a week of this.

What a surprise it was at Christmas when Santa brought me a Lionel train set; track, engine, cars, and model station. Dad helped me put everything together and explained the workings of the transformer. I was the happiest kid in the neighborhood. I quickly learned if a train engine or car derailed off the track, I had to crawl over and reset it. Mom and Dad made clear that it was my job to correct the speed outcomes.

In January 1954, Dad was elected chairman of the Knox County, Illinois, chapter of the National Foundation for Infantile Paralysis, which later became known as the March of Dimes. The committee worked through most of 1954 to collect a total of about five thousand dollars for the organization—a large sum of money in those days.

Throughout 1954, I continued to be as mobile as I could, exercising with my mother's supervision and direction, as well as playing with my sister Kendra. I would put the dolls that she got for Christmas on the railroad tracks and hit them with the train engine. She didn't think this was as funny as I did.

I was able to enjoy playing with my childhood friends inside and outside the house in limited amounts. Activities outside were assisted by the use of an old wooden wheelchair, similar to the one President Franklin D. Roosevelt (FDR) used after he was stricken with polio. Of course, it weighed more than I did. The neighborhood kids enjoyed pushing me in the wheelchair and typically had a few accidents going over street curbs or running into bushes. They all seemed to enjoy watching me during these accidents. Playing in sandboxes was always fun until I got sand on my legs, which worked its way down inside the casts. It was like wearing heavy socks made out of sandpaper. It was no surprise, as active as I was, that the casts had to be removed and replaced with newer ones due to the damage they'd incurred. Of course, new signatures and pictures were penned on them each time.

Near the end of 1955 I was once again looking forward to a train ride to Chicago. The purpose of this trip was to plan extensive surgery on both legs and figure out what should be done prior to the surgery and what the expectations would be for afterward. We met with Dr. McElvenny at his office and discussed the surgical plan, the bilateral hamstring transplant intended for both left and right legs. Dr. Gene Caldwell of Louisiana would assist in the surgical procedures. Both doctors knew each other from college and respected each other. Naturally, Mom understood what they were talking about and was supportive of the plan. If I had actually known what they were plotting, I am sure I would have voted no!

Not long after my fifth birthday, on January 21, 1956, the first surgical procedure was performed on my left leg with a full cast applied to protect and secure full knee extension. The procedure lasted approximately nine hours. I was informed that everything went very well afterward and I would be in the hospital for a few weeks for some needed rest and cast drying. The one challenge doctors did not fully explain to me was the application of two cardboard tubes, one on each arm, to prevent me from bending my arms to scratch or try to remove this large chunk of plaster on my leg. I am sure I cried a lot trying to remove those tubes so I could get to the cast.

March 12, 1956, came around and I was told they were going to remove the cast. They needed to check the two surgical sites on my left leg. What they didn't tell me was that a partial cast would be reapplied. Just my luck. As I recovered, Gail Bullis, a close family friend, was gracious enough to mail me postcards with a riddle question one day, and then the answer the next day. This continued throughout all the times I was in the hospital.

May 14 of that year brought another journey to Chicago, to have a wedging cast applied to my right leg; things just kept getting better. I spent a lot of time in the large wooden wheelchair, being pushed around by the nurses. I watched (on a black-and-white television) shows like: *Ding Dong School*, *Garfield Goose and Friends*, and *Kukla, Fran and Ollie* on Chicago's WGN-TV from the hospital playroom. In a short time, I mastered the art of moving the wheelchair, much to the nurse's dismay. I can remember not liking the dinners, composed of salmon patties, yellow beans, and worst of all, cooked spinach. With all of the beds in the pediatric ward full, there was little time to ask for different food. The bright spot every day was when the nurses brought around bedtime snacks, like Salerno butter cookies, served as a reward for the evening meal. To this day, I still do not like salmon patties, yellow beans, or cooked spinach. But I love the cookies.

I can still remember the daily routine in the hospital: nurses checking every couple of hours during the night, bed pans, morning breakfast, and a bed bath. An afternoon nap or visitors followed lunch. Family and friends with toys would travel the one hundred fifty miles from Galesburg to see me. I was blessed to have quite a few visitors make the trip. I also remember occasionally getting a cup of Neapolitan ice cream. I'm not sure why, perhaps to distract me from pain, or I was being rewarded for being a great patient.

The surgery on my right leg was scheduled for May 26, 1956, at Wesley Memorial Hospital. Naturally, this meant another enjoyable train ride in the Denver Zephyr's Vista Dome car. On this trip I had toys that I could play with: tricky dogs, which were two separate magnets, and a Whee-lo, which was a red plastic wheel with axles that moved inside of a bent frame of metal. The trick with the Whee-lo was to keep the red wheel within the control of the frame. I found myself searching around for the wheel many times. To this day, I believe Mom purchased that toy so I would get exercise.

By this time, I was starting to remember more and, of course, ask questions. During my second nine-hour surgery I recall waking up and starting to lift my head on the operating room table, wondering why the doctors and nurses were looking at me so oddly. That moment was a brief second.

Instantly, a wire mask with gauze was brought to my face. It had a horrible smell, and I was asleep in a split second. Then I remember waking up back in my room. I drifted in and out of sleep for what seemed like hours. No matter how hard I tried, I was not able to stay awake; it was scary. During the night the nurses kept coming in, turning on lights that had a blue glow and bothering me with pills, a rectal thermometer, a cold bedpan, and water to drink.

The following morning, Mom appeared. I assumed she was there all night, but I wasn't awake enough to know. She explained the waking-up incident in surgery the day before and told me it was the ether that put me right back to sleep. Ether was used those days as anesthesia. It smelled like nail polish remover, which was not allowed in our house, ever. I appreciated her explaining it to me, but what it meant really didn't register until many years later.

It seemed like Mom was always around while I was in the hospital. I know she stayed at a hotel on Michigan Avenue. I can't really recall how many days a week she was there, but it seemed like every day. I was always wondering why the other children in the pediatric ward did not have the visitors that I was lucky enough to get. Mom would hold me up by the window so I could look out and see lots of tall buildings, Lake Michigan, and the electric streetcars down below. Chicago was larger and a lot different from my hometown. Many years later, as I was growing into adulthood, I still felt bad for those children who did not have visitors, and I was always curious how that affected them mentally and physically.

As with the previous surgery, I was blessed with a full

leg cast. It felt like a bag of cement was on my leg. Later that year, the full leg cast was removed and a shorter wedging cast was applied. Lucky for me, it was removed by September for the start of first grade at Silas Willard Grade School, in Galesburg. It was the same grade school President Ronald Reagan had attended as a child.

3

STARTING SCHOOL

*"Attacking people with disabilities is the
lowest display of power I can think of."*

—Morgan Freeman

September 1956 brought the first day of school for my
neighborhood buddies and me. Mom or Dad took a picture of me, Kendra, Eddie Dunlop, and Marc Bullis as we
were preparing to go to school. I did not have any idea
what this was going to be all about. The other kids walked
to school while Mom gave me a ride and walked with me
into the building, to show me my classroom and where
the bathrooms were. I think I even met the school nurse.
I don't recall thinking a lot about how I walked and how
careful I had to be getting into my desk or going up and
down stairs.

It took a while for our neighborhood group to realize the classroom was not a playroom, but we would get
thirty minutes of recess in the morning and after lunch.

The playground had teeter-totters and a jungle gym. The playground was covered with coal cinders from the burnt coal furnace, small loose particles that were painful when you fell on them. For most of the school year my time outside was spent watching kids participate in a lot of different activities: kickball, dodge ball, and chasing each other around to burn off energy. I never thought much about the fact that I was on the sidelines. To me, it was just the way life was.

I got to meet the school nurse again one afternoon after falling down in the hall on both knees, on an incline. Of course, she called Mom to have her come by the school. Mom in turn called our family doctor and had him meet her there. My right knee hurt the worst, but I had pain and abrasions on both knees. They decided I should wear kneepads, so when I fell again, I would have a little protection. Mom started teaching me how to fall to avoid damage to my knees. Wearing kneepads under my jeans made getting my jeans on difficult, and once they were on, the kneepads really restricted bending my knees to sit, stand, or walk. Having to bend my knees when sitting with the pads made my knee joint hurt and caused abrasions. Trying to soften the pain with a wrapping of cotton gauze made it worse. This new addition to my wardrobe continued until I was through the sixth grade. But by the end of the school year I was at least able to walk around much better and participate, to a small extent, with the other kids in playground activities.

One of the best times in a child's life is when school lets out for the summer, and this would be the first summer

I'd be able to really enjoy the outdoors with my friends. I was under strict house rules to limit any activities that could cause me to fall and potentially do damage to what the surgeries had fixed. Most of our playtime was around our house and patio. I'm sure this was prearranged by my mom and other mothers in the neighborhood.

Mom and Dad rented an FDR wooden wheelchair for use outside at $12.50 a month. The chair was large and heavy, and the wheels were difficult for me to propel. I'm guessing this was also preplanned, but I finally figured out that if I moved from side to side, I could reach one wheel at a time and go forward, primarily in a zigzag pattern. My friends thought it was fun to push me in the wheelchair and scare me. What are friends for? On rainy days or really hot days we stayed inside the house, either sliding down the steps (like on the sled), watching TV (in black and white, of course), or playing with a variety of toys, with the number-one attraction being the train set. During the times my casts were off Mom would exercise my legs by placing a sandbag under each heel and pressing on my knees for full extension to stretch the transplanted muscles. This was not a fun process to experience three times each day.

In August 1957, Mom and I took another train ride back to Chicago to visit the doctor and see some landmarks. We went to the Field Museum of Natural History, the Shedd Aquarium, and Grant Park. The museums overwhelmed me, especially the dinosaurs at the Field Museum. It was hard to picture something that big walking around the Earth. I had the same feelings when I saw all the big fish in the aquarium. Mom took me by the Allerton Hotel, to show me where she stayed when I was in the hospital. We even had lunch at the Palmer House, which I would visit many years later. Our tour was in a yellow taxi; it seemed like a large truck with a very friendly driver. I cannot imagine how many train trips Mom made from Galesburg to Chicago over the years when I was in the hospital. I'm not even going to try to guess.

When we finally got to the doctor's office, Mom and the doctor thought it would be best to put wedging casts on each leg again for about two and a half months before school started. My guess is that they were concerned about my increased activity and wanted a layer of protection other than the kneepads. The good news was that it wasn't a hot summer, so the casts wouldn't feel like an oven.

School would be starting soon but I would not be going back to Silas Willard Grade School for a while. It was decided that I would start second grade at Lillian Taylor School, for children with disabilities. Although I got to visit the school before the school year started, I was scared about what was going to happen and when I would see my friends again. On the first day, a small bus picked me up, wheelchair and all, at home and dropped me off at school. I couldn't understand why there were so many children there with different physical limitations. My only memory of that day is taking naps on a rug in the morning and in the afternoon. I guess I wanted to erase the rest of the memories. School was out for the day earlier there than other schools, so the bus would have me home before my friends. Those few months were horrible. These kids were not like my friends back home, and even though I was there only for a couple months until the casts were removed, I told Mom I never wanted to go back. I was very concerned that I would be there again in the future.

Fortunately, I was soon in Chicago for a checkup and to remove the casts. Then it was back to Galesburg and back to my friends in second grade at Silas Willard Grade School. With permission to participate in a little more activity on the playground, I took full advantage. I had to make up for lost time. Falling down on the coal cinders was always painful, but it was even worse trying to stand up. There was virtually no grip for my feet to be secure. Having to crawl to a spot where I could pull myself up made for tears and dirt on my pants. I wanted to get on the jungle gym and climb all over it. The teachers would not let me do it, as they were scared I would fall and break something. As soon as they turned their backs on me and looked away, I tried to climb to the top but realized I didn't have the leg strength; I still enjoyed being around the kids and grabbing them as they climbed around.

The merry-go-round was another experience. Some kids stood on it, but I had to sit, and when the older kids saw me on it, they thought it was going to be fun to spin it around fast and see how long I could stay on without falling off. Good news: there were no small coal cinders nearby. Of course, the teacher scolded the older kids numerous times for doing this, but I still got back on the merry-go-round and played with them.

Once school was out for the summer, we looked forward to "trying" to stay out of trouble. The neighborhood group developed its own rules for football and baseball so I could participate and not be injured. Playing with the army men we had received and collected from Christmas and birthdays was a good sit-down project for us. Marbles, mumbley-peg (played with a pocketknife), and jacks kept us busy both as a group and individually. We also realized the fun of chalk drawing on sidewalks and driveways; however, our parents did not enjoy this as much as we did. We used to get balsa wood airplanes to assemble from the local neighbor drugstore; we spent a lot of time throwing them around and trying to modify them so they'd go further. When we were done playing with them, we realized we could actually put charcoal lighter fluid on each one, light a match, and watch them almost fly while burning. That happened on a few occasions. We tried to blame a lightning strike but our parents were a lot smarter than we were.

In the evenings as the sun set, we learned how to catch fireflies and put them in a mason jar or turn them into rings for our fingers. Cruel, but fun. We also learned there was a bug that shed its hard skin in late summer. That skin was stiff and great to scare the neighborhood girls with, so we really collected a lot of those katydid shells.

Most neighborhoods had a bully who would harass kids, push them down, and throw water balloons at them. Our neighborhood was no exception. Our bully's initials were D. S. and I was his victim most of the time. I was always the easy target, a slow walker and easy to shove over. (My immobility got me into a lot of trouble, actually. I was unable to leave an area when we pulled a prank on somebody—my escape time was very slow. Mom and Dad got a lot of phone calls from neighbors, filling them in on what we had done.) When we walked home, we would always have to go by D. S.'s house, which set the stage for harassment and what we called "fights." My best friend, Marc Bullis, tried to intervene one day when D. S. pushed me down. Marc attempted to do the same thing to D. S.; however, that fell short of success and Marc went down. When I got home from school on those days, I told Mom and Dad what had happened. Mom encouraged me to walk away when those situations came up. Dad, however, told me to strike back because I had the upper arm strength to protect myself.

4

THIRD GRADE

"However difficult life may seem, there is always something you can do and succeed at."

—Stephen Hawking

Late summer arrived and it was time for another train trip to Chicago. I still enjoyed the ride from Galesburg to Chicago. It was really an experience to see the small towns and farms pass by. Arriving in Chicago was a whole other world with buildings, skyscrapers, bridges, and lots of roadways teeming with cars. As we approached and entered Union Station, all of a sudden it seemed like nighttime. We were in a tunnel, moving at a very slow pace for a long time. Then the train stopped, and we saw people walking or running up and down the concrete walkway, arriving or leaving. When we got off the train, we would go down this cold, dark, noisy walkway to the station, which had hundreds and hundreds of people, little cafés, lots of stairs, rows and rows of large wood benches, gift shops, and really tall ceilings. Outside the station we approached what appeared to be a large garage full of taxicabs parked all over. It seemed that Mom knew a couple of the porters who would help her with her suitcase and get me into the cab. I always enjoyed their hospitality and respect. On the return trip to Galesburg the view was the same, but I always tried to find scenes I hadn't noticed on the way into Chicago.

I was checked in to Wesley Memorial Hospital to have my legs x-rayed and to have new wedging casts applied. This was going to be a short visit and we would be heading home in a few days. My two new wedging casts were to stay on for a longer period of time, however. I was beginning to wonder if this was going to be a yearly occurrence. The day after we got back Mom and Dad explained that I would be at home for the first part of third grade. A teacher, Mrs. Sterling, had been employed to homeschool me for about a month or so; then I could return to Silas Willard Grade School to be with my friends. I didn't really care for this idea, but it was on Mom's and the doctors' orders.

I never really did like studying, and the homeschooling didn't impress me one bit. On the bright side, though, I knew Dad had been building a large platform system for the expansion of my Lionel train set in the basement. When the train set was done it comprised four engines, one hundred and fifty cars, two levels, a retractable drawbridge, a farm site with buildings, a village with the train station, and train yards to park the additional engines and cars. Dad even wired old Christmas tree lights into the building and houses. Needless to say, all my friends adored it. It was difficult to try to pay attention to Mrs. Sterling and her attempts to homeschool me with a large train set calling my name from downstairs.

By mid-November I was back in school with my friends, just in time to learn how to walk and play in snow, carefully. We made trips around the county to sled on what few hills there were in our corner of Illinois. Of course, I was to stay off the hills that were really long and high, for obvious reasons, but it was fun anyway. Marc Bullis's father, Tom, would take us out on quiet country roads with our sleds and pull us on the snow behind his car. We thought we were going one hundred miles per hour when, in fact, it was probably closer to five or ten. I was only able to participate in that adventure one time. Mom had a long talk with Tom and that was the last time I was asked to go.

When spring arrived, Dad installed a basketball hoop and backboard on the garage. I'm not sure if it was for him or for me to play with, but he was out there quite a bit with me. Most of the time I walked around the court to shoot, I would fall because my knees buckled. I cannot guess how many large Band-Aids we went through that summer. I even had a lesson from Dad on how to weave the basketball net when he made a hoop pattern out of a round piece of plywood. It was fun and I got it done, but my patience was never enough to do something like that long term.

After the basketball hoop-weaving lesson, Dad wanted to build a brick fireplace in the backyard for burning trash and roasting hot dogs. I was to be his right-hand man and learn how to mix concrete and carry bricks. Halfway through laying the bricks, one of the bricks I handed to him landed on his thumb. That was the first time I heard my father cry out in pain. We went back up to the house and Dad showed me where the bruise and the blood were collecting under his fingernail. Much to my surprise, he got out a small drill and had me help him drill through the thumbnail so the blood would not keep collecting underneath. I was never sure if this was a lesson or payback for dropping the brick.

After the brick-dropping incident, Mom informed me that I would be taking piano lessons. You can imagine how I felt about that. For the first lesson Mom and I walked about three blocks to the piano teacher's house. She introduced me to the teacher, who said the lessons would be about thirty minutes, which seemed more like three days to me. After the boring lesson my walk home took me past the small house of an elderly lady who loved to make cinnamon rolls. I found out that Mrs. McGahee would bake them every Saturday. It smelled like walking through a large bakery as bread was coming out of the oven. Mom encouraged me to go buy a few of these large cinnamon buns the next Saturday. I could never determine why I, and not my sister, was always sent on this errand until years later, when I heard it was Mom's plan for me. Something about exercise. The piano lessons lasted about two weeks, when the teacher called Mom and informed her that I had no musical talent. That ended that.

Mom and Dad had close friends with a cabin on nearby Lake Bracken. They decided I should start learning how to fish, which sounded like a lot of fun to me. I think it was more about them getting together with their friends. The first fishing trip was interesting. The cabin was up on a hill a short distance from the lake. To get to the boat, I had to walk down the hill, a new challenge for me. Walking down a hill was a difficult task—my knees wanted to buckle. I didn't have strength or flexibility in my knees going downhill. So: more grass and dirt stains on my pants. Getting into the boat itself was scary. When I left the dock to get in, the boat started to rock back and forth, causing me to lose my balance and fall on one of the seats. The fishing was poor and I got bored, so we went back to the cabin and called it a day. They decided the next time we went fishing we would use the pontoon boat, which would be more stable and safer for me.

5

MORE ADVENTURES

*"The only thing worse than being blind is
having sight but no vision."*

—Helen Keller

Cub Scouts was to be my next adventure. Marc Bullis and
I joined a troop, wore the blue uniforms with scarves, and
enjoyed the programs with our new friends. Each week we
were to do a new project and explain how we completed
it at the following meeting. It was a fun thing to see what
our new friends had accomplished and to share ideas.
Marc and I stayed with the Cub Scouts for two years and
earned our Webelos badges. The journey from my house
to the scoutmaster's house was about two blocks on sidewalks that were old and cracked, so it was another walking challenge with numerous falls, thanks for the irritating
kneepads. (Many years later, as an adult, I acted as a Boy
Scouts of America regional chairman for the district of
about three thousand Scouts.)

I was also excited to start the fourth grade, seeing both my old friends and new friends from the Cub Scout troop. Walking a block and a half to and from school seemed to be getting easier with fewer falls. As annoying as the kneepads were, I felt less pain when I did fall. Mom added a new program this year, for more exercise. I was to walk her friend's daughter, Marsie, home from school and she would pick me up at her house. The walk to Marsie's house was about three and half blocks, with four different intersections to cross. Aside from the delight of being able to walk with a cute young girl in my class, her mother always had chocolate chip cookies or, my favorite, chocolate ice cream cake waiting.

My dear mother and Marc's mother, Gail Bullis, plotted a spring and summer plan for me. I found myself in charge of lawn mowing for our house and the Bullis house. Never mind that there were four kids in the Bullis family and I had an older sister. Any of them could have mowed, but I accepted the challenge for $1.25 per week total for both lawns. It took years for me to reflect back on these tasks and their purpose. To this day, I am truly thankful for my parents and their friends' creative planning.

In May of that year, I got to take another train trip to Chicago, enjoying the Vista Dome car, Union Station, and the walk through the terminal to the taxicabs again. Walking seemed easier, except for a few spots on the terrazzo floor that were wet and slippery. While I was looking at all of the people and shops, I wasn't paying attention to where I was stepping.

The news at the doctor's office was unexpected, but I took it in stride given the other procedures I'd had up to that time: because I was actively walking with more pressure on my big toes, putting stress on them, the doctor was concerned I could possibly fracture them. I had been walking that way, not having my heel hit the ground first, so that had been cause for concern for falls. Once again, surgery was scheduled.

The procedure would fuse each big toe and the toe next to it with steel pins that would stick out the top of each toe under plaster leg casts. The long leg casts were to force and continue full extension of my knees so that the transplanted muscles would stay at normal extension. At the far end of the casts, around my ankles and feet, the casts had a wide thick loop that went over my big toes. Under those were stainless steel pins put in the first two toes, to fuse those joints and make them stronger.

The plaster toe loops did not survive the abuse they got. As luck would have it, it was a hot summer and the activities I had become accustomed to would be on the back burner for about three months. I amused myself and the other kids in the neighborhood by letting them push me in an old wooden wheelchair with these two steel pins sticking straight out of my toes. Mom was not really happy when the wheelchair tipped over with me in it. No damage was done but the neighborhood kids got scolded for pushing me in the wheelchair. We then had lemonade and cookies on our patio. I did see a grin on Mom's face; she understood how boys play.

In winter the casts came off. It was time to get back to a safe walking routine, and it was time for snowmen and snowball fights. Because I'd been a cheap resource for mowing the lawn, Mom also volunteered me to shovel the driveway and sidewalks. By the way, the corner lot we lived on had twice the number of sidewalks to shovel. Lots of slips and falls that winter, so another life lesson learned in walking and balance.

My ego was bruised, but I got over it by spring, when I enrolled in the YMCA and went every Saturday with my church basketball team, swimming and walking around the track on the second floor. The goal of my position on the basketball team was to draw fouls. My trainers' (parents') new plan was to have me walk the mile to the YMCA, and when I was done, I was to walk to Dad's office, at least another mile. We would then ride home together and stop for lunch sometimes. To get to his office I had to cross a large set of railroad tracks, about four sets in the crossing. I was scared to death because I knew I would not be able to run if I saw a train coming. The tracks made for a surface similar to rows of corn. The Burlington Northern tracks carried about seventy-five trains a day through Galesburg. Hearing the whistles in the distance scared me. Still to this day, I get concerned about crossing railroad tracks, even in a car.

6

WALKING

"Never ignore somebody with a disability.
You don't realize how much they can inspire you."

—Unknown

I began fifth grade in 1959. There were no wedging casts that summer, but I was to keep doing knee exercises twice a day. Just like in years before, I would sit on the floor with my legs out, put a beanbag under my heel, and push my knee down as close to the floor as possible. In addition, I would bend at the waist to get my nose to the floor to stretch entire leg muscles. Thank goodness I didn't have leg casts! This exercise routine was the same one Mom had performed on me three times a day since Day One, when there were no casts.

Marc and I would occasionally leave school for lunch and walk a block and a half to North Side Bakery, where we would eat and buy candy before heading back. On other days we would just stop at the bakery, get some cookies, and then go back to school. There was an old candy store in another direction; it had lots of steps, so I avoided it. The streets were made of a brick material known as Purington Pavers. These were basically large bricks with their name raised on the top of each paver. The street pavers in our neighborhood were put down in the early 1900s. The curbs were 8' x 8' x 6' granite blocks, which made for a very high threshold when crossing the street. Mother Nature does what she does best, moving the curbs and pavers with the thaw in the spring. Naturally, this made walking and bike riding a little tricky. When I was just learning how to ride a bike, there were lots of bumps, bruises, scrapes, and Band-Aids.

I was still in charge of mowing yards as I had been in previous years, for the same rate. My friends played football and softball in the yards while I was mowing, which didn't really bother me. I felt comfortable walking behind something that I was pushing, and watching them play increased my self-confidence and stability. The neighborhood group caught on to the fact that I was unable to run, so they dreamed up a couple of pranks that would get me in trouble while they had fun. One of our neighbors had a large clump of bushes in his backyard, with a large space in the middle. We, or should I say, the group decided it would be cool to smoke a cigarette in the bushes. One of the guys got some cigarettes (we never asked him from where but we were sure he didn't pay for them), and we took off for the bushes. We had no idea how to smoke a cigarette, but we knew we had to light the end with matches. We attempted to smoke one, but actually it was more like lighting a cigarette and watching it burn. There was a lot of coughing, however. We heard somebody coming near us, asking what was going on in the bushes. That triggered the group, with the exception of me, to scram. Not being able to run, I was the one who got in trouble and the event was reported to my mother.

Sometime before school started, this same group of little rascals took fireworks and went to Silas Willard Grade School to shoot them off in the playground. Well, I got suckered again. Three of my friends decided they would go in the back door of the school and look around. I told them I would just stay out in back. Shortly after that, I heard a whole package of fireworks going off inside the building and I knew I was in trouble, no surprise. Those three little rascals ran out the front door and headed home. I got to talk to the custodian and he, in turn, got to talk with my mom. Lesson learned: don't put yourself in a position where you'd need to run if you can't. I still stick by that to this day.

Confirmation classes at Trinity Lutheran Church in Galesburg were coming to a conclusion. Some of us boys were involved in the Sunday service for a few months as acolytes, lighting the candles, preparing the wine and wafers, and bringing them to the altar. It was very regimented, from the time to be at church to the dress code to the service expectations of handling the offerings collection and putting out the candles' flames. I enjoyed the duties with the exception of carrying the wine tray and the fully poured glasses. The trip from the prep room to the altar required me to walk up three separate high steps over the course of about fifty feet. Not being very smooth in walk-ing, some of the wine spilled on my white robe. Another life lesson: do not fill glasses to the brim, which, by the way, I quit doing when I was twenty-one years old.

Again, my mom volunteered me to do something. I took over a newspaper route when an older neighbor boy was going on vacation with his family. As I remember, there were about sixty papers on the route. The first day, Dad drove me to the houses, and I walked the papers up to each front door. From that day on, I was on my own, folding the papers and then either walking with a heavy canvas bag or using my bike. Thank goodness there was no snow or rain. I got to be a good shot with the papers and hitting squirrels.

Halloween came around and, of course, we had to walk around, ringing doorbells or knocking to get candy apples, popcorn balls, and anything else offered for treats. Wearing a costume and carrying a paper bag with apples, candy bars, and such was quite difficult while traversing the sidewalks and corner crossings in the dark. So, I called it quits after about a block up one side and down the other. I found out a couple days later that my friends had con-tinued their trick-or-treating journey and got their bags completely full. They had told the homeowners they were also getting treats for Dick Hardine because it was hard for him to walk. And do you think those rascals shared any of those goodies? The answer is no, but they were still my friends.

After Halloween there were a few warm days and Dad thought we should go fishing at Lake Bracken. I agreed that would be fun. I was awakened at 4:30 the following morning because "You can't get there too early for the fish." My dad and I fished for a while off a dock and then we moved to another spot on the lakeshore and caught a few catfish before we quit. My hands smelled horrible from the catfish bait. Dad thought it was funny. I did not. On the way back home, Dad drove me through a YMCA camp in the woods on the lakeshore and told me stories of when he had been there many years before. They had cabins, a theater area, campfire rings, a dining hall, outdoor bathrooms, and the most important thing, a canteen store where you could get candy and T-shirts. (More candy than shirts were sold, I'm sure.)

Dad asked me if I would like to go to the camp for two weeks the following summer and I said that would be fun. Well, I found out in early spring that to go to camp I had to sell a number of boxes of saltwater taffy. I somehow agreed to do that. What I did not realize was that the saltwater boxes came in cases of twenty-five boxes each, with no handles. They probably weighed about twenty-five pounds each.

Not being good on a bicycle with a large box meant that I had to walk around the neighborhood, knock on doors, and try to get people to buy the taffy. I seemed to continually get into situations where I had to walk a lot and carry things. Of course, I knew who was responsible for that: Mom and Dad. They had that plan for me. I mentioned this camp to my friend Marc and he thought it would be fun to go, but he opted out of selling the candy and got his dad to just pay for the two weeks.

There was a lot to do at camp—crafts, canoeing, using an outhouse for the first time, swimming, searching for snakes, hiking, and sitting around campfires listening to stories. I guess because I had been in the hospital so many times before without any family around me, it didn't really bother me to not see my family while at camp. I didn't miss home like some of the other campers did. Marc decided it was not for him and left after two days; he still hears about that.

Camp was another lesson in walking up and down hills over rocks and trees. Getting up from a fall there was as difficult as falling in the playground at grade school or on snow. Mom was on the swimming and diving team in college, so naturally, swimming was going to be on my activity list. At Lake Bracken she'd taught me to swim, and with her training, I won three first-place ribbons at camp, two in back stroke and one in breaststroke, and a second-place ribbon in freestyle. I also got a black eye when a kid jumped in the water and hit my head near my nose, but the first- and second-place ribbons made it worthwhile.

The YMCA had two overnight road trips that year to Saint Louis and Chicago, to see major league baseball games. The old stadiums posed some mobility issues on stairs and other uneven surfaces, but I felt proud of myself negotiating the steps and I was excited to get home and tell Mom and Dad. A visit to Chicago's famous Riverview Amusement Park was not so much fun. The ride on the roller coaster was very scary—the ups, downs, and turns scared me to death. That experience was the first and last time I went on that ride.

7

JUNIOR HIGH SCHOOL

"Focus not on the differences of people with disabilities but the talent of the individual."

—Neil Milliken

The time had come for me to go to junior high school. I would start the seventh grade with hundreds of new classmates. The classes were in different rooms, not just one like grade school. Homeroom was the first class, for announcements and roll call, and then the day started. A bell would ring and you had only a few minutes to get to the next class. If you were late, you got put on the tardy list. This was the new routine, class to class to lunch to class, etc. Having to carry all my books to school in the morning and sorting them out in my locker between each class accounted for me falling, picking up my books from the floor, and being tardy many times. I'm glad I had kneepads.

Lunch was a new experience as well. Unlike the ease of carrying a bag of cookies and candy from the bakery, carrying a full tray of food was difficult. While carrying my tray I had to watch my step, keep my balance, and look out for trip hazards. Safe mobility was a minor issue since I was used to falling. The good news was there were no stairs.

Churchill Junior High School was composed of kids who had gone to eight grade schools on the north side of Galesburg. The south-side kids went to another school, Lombard Junior High School. I realized I was not the only student with a physical handicap at Churchill. The other student, Lester, was in the eighth-grade class. He had cerebral palsy. He used a wheelchair with different types of attachments and had someone available to push him class to class. He had trouble speaking, but we did notice each other and tried to communicate the best we could. Churchill Junior High School also had a separate classroom for kids with special needs; the "developmentally disabled." However, the higher functioning students would attend a few of the regular classes such as gym and industrial arts.

These experiences were new to me and my self-image seemed to change a little for the better. Other kids would make fun of the developmentally disabled and tease them. That was hard for me to understand, as they could not respond to the teasing or understand it. I really felt sad for them. I was bullied by a boy in my class, but not like the second-grade bullying; this was more physical. He would walk behind me when going to a class, call me a derogatory name, and then hit me in the back. After a week of putting up with his hitting, things changed. We had rounded a corner in between classes when he called me a name before he hit me. I turned around and punched him in the face. His nose bled, and I smiled. The bad news was, it happened in front of the art teacher who I did not notice until I turned back around, grinning. I knew I was in trouble. She took a swing at me with one of her wooden crutches and I went down. The teacher in the next room helped me get up since there was nothing for me to grab to pull myself up.

Later, I learned the art teacher had also had polio years before, not that it was an excuse. The other student and I were both sent to the to the principal's office. He saw the school nurse first. While he deserved it, I should not have hit him. That said, nobody had seen the hits I had been getting. Because he was known to be a bully, he was suspended from school for three days and I got two days. When Mom came to get me, she wasn't happy that I hadn't walked away from him. Mom always said to walk away from a fight; it would make the other person madder. However, when Dad was home from work, he was on my side and had the opposite thought. My, how the times change. The art teacher with crutches, Miss Wiggins, and I avoided each other for the next few years.

The coming spring was the start of the baseball season. Dad and his friend Jack thought it would be a good idea if I joined a hardball league in Galesburg— the Knights of Columbus, a Catholic team. With Jack's help, they brought me onto the team as batboy and fill-in third baseman. I thought this was strange. Knowing that I could not run, why would they want me on a hardball team? Perhaps it was an excuse for Dad and Jack to socialize with each other and their wives while I exercised. I was apprehensive about being on the team and unable to participate in the game itself. On a couple of occasions, when the team was ahead in the scoring, they let me play third base. It took a few times for me to realize I could still enjoy the game and the players and accept my limits, since they were ahead anyway.

After the team's season was over, I was enlisted to help a family friend on his farm, loading hay onto a hay wagon. We used the old-fashioned method; lift from field, throw on wagon. This was more work than my legs could handle, even though I was lucky enough to be on the hay wagon to catch and stack. Lesson learned: loose hay on a hay wagon is slippery and equals falling.

The next two years were uneventful—no falls or fights. I was just focused on getting to know my teachers and other kids. My summers included vacations with Mom, Dad, and Kendra to Gatlinburg, Tennessee, and Saint Louis, Missouri. On the trip to Gatlinburg, we decided to use a ski lift so we could enjoy the view of the Great Smoky Mountains from the top. But as the lift was about to make its turn to go down, I fell off the seat. Getting off the lift was difficult; when it is rocking at the normal speed, you need to jump and run from the seat. I was unable to accomplish either, so I went down on both knees to the gravel; pain and abrasions, Band-Aids. Lesson learned: stay off ski lifts. To this day, I stay away from rocking chairs.

The number of vacation days we had was always based on Dad's work schedule. He was the chief civil engineer for a large road and bridge construction company in western Illinois. I spent a lot of time with Dad fishing on Saturdays and going with him to construction sites and then breakfast so he could plan the next week's schedule for his crews. On one Saturday Dad was to survey a large piece of land for a new housing subdivision. As luck would have it, I got to go with him and learn how to survey. Of course, Dad got the easy part with the tripod and transit, while I was sent out into the field with the elevation pole. There were bumps, and with the grass growing, walking proved difficult for me. There were quite a few times when my knees would buckle and I would go to the ground. I again realized that I was still walking more on my toes than on my heels. The heel should've hit the ground first, allowing me to lock my knees.

The summer before high school started, a new country club, Lake Lawn Swim and Tennis Club, opened up in town. I was offered a job as junior lifeguard and deckhand. Aside from being a lifeguard, my other duties included cleaning the pool, putting out chairs, cleaning the filter mechanisms, working in the locker room, and distributing clothes from baskets. Other assignments would come up, like working in the snack bar making lunches for people, keeping the clubhouse clean, and a new sport for me: teaching archery. I was no Robin Hood but it was a lot of fun. It was a wonderful summer with new friends, girls in bathing suits, and getting a nice tan.

With the job three miles from home, I had to either walk or ride my bike; I choose the bike. The one problem I experienced was that I could no longer wear kneepads because they weren't in style with a swimsuit. After years of wearing them, I stopped. With the different levels of concrete around the pool for water draining, my knees buckled a number of times. I went down and had some pretty serious abrasions on my right knee. Embarrassing, but a part of life. This incident, along with the way I walked, did nothing for my self-image or popularity with girls.

About a month before school was to start at Galesburg Senior High School, I had fallen a couple more times. The first time required seven stitches in my right knee. Wouldn't you know it, two weeks later it happened again, on the same knee, so I was back to the emergency room. Our family doctor convinced Mom (who happened to be the director of nursing service at the hospital) that I should learn to be more careful. So, their plan was to let me sew up my own knee. I was a little unsure but thought, *What the heck? After it's numb, it shouldn't be such a big deal.* After I got used to putting the needle through the skin, it got a lot easier, not that I would want to ever do that again. One more lesson learned.

8

HIGH SCHOOL YEARS

"It's not our disabilities, it's our abilities that count."
—Chris Burke

Galesburg Senior High School was significantly larger than my junior high school building, with large wide stairwells from the first floor to the second floor. Going up one seemed like climbing a mountain. With my leg weakness, I always went down the steps backward. You can imagine the jokes that came, so I would wait till the steps were clear and be the last one down. We had the same routine as in junior high: homeroom; bell ringing signaling the next class; move fast and try to pay attention. The sophomore class was composed of about 580 kids. It was quite an increase from twenty-five kids per class in grade school and two hundred in junior high. The attitude and temperament of the class was a lot different. The boys and the girls fought for popularity.

Gym class wasn't in my schedule for obvious reasons. Instead I was recruited to be the basketball team's manager.

I had to wear a shirt and tie to the games, and my duties included cleaning, polishing basketballs, keeping score, and making sure the team had what it needed for road trips. I had the desire to try wrestling; I watched the team practice and thought, *With my upper arm strength, I could do that.* I found myself participating in their practice sessions but not the matches so I could avoid the take down and possible damage to either leg. I had great upper extremity strength and did well once we were on the gym mat. Mom did not want me on the team, so this was next best thing.

About halfway through the school year I'd made a lot of new friends who were fun and considerate of my abilities. As a young man, I was always curious about girls, dating, and how they would accept my physical abilities. Jini was a very attractive girl in a few of my classes. I had a hard time getting up the nerve to talk to her, let alone ask her out. But I met her at her locker one day and did it, and she said yes! Of course, I needed a driver, so my sister Kendra and her boyfriend picked us up. No surprise, they teased me the whole time. A taxi would have been less annoying. We went to a James Bond movie; I was embarrassed about the girls in the movie, so we left. To this day I feel bad about picking that particular movie, though Jini and I still stay in contact and talk about it. The fact that she still liked me even though I'd made a mistake provided me with a great improvement in my self-image and self-confidence, a feeling I thought I would never have.

There were a few bullies in high school, but they never bothered me. Some of their fights actually required a few teachers to break them up. As the year progressed, I found myself falling more. Thank goodness for Mom's lessons on bracing myself.

With the end of the school year came another trip to address my mobility issues, by car this time. Dr. McElvenny, who had performed outstanding surgery on me over the years, had passed away a year before. His office referred us to Dr. James Ahstrom at West Suburban Hospital in Oak Park, a suburb west of Chicago. After he evaluated me medically and reviewed my history, he decided that corrective surgery on both feet should go forward, to decrease my falling and improve my walking. *Here we go again.* Both doctors who had successfully performed the initial hamstring transplants recommended that I look for a career that would provide me with a desk. They were concerned with my future strength and mobility.

The new procedure was called a triple arthrodesis, with a lengthening of the Achilles heel tendon. Or more simply put, the surgery would lengthen my heel cord, fusing the bones in the arch of each foot so I would have stiffer feet and longer Achilles tendons. This would allow for heel-to-toe walking. Unfortunately, this would end my basketball manager career at Galesburg Senior High School.

After the surgery and a ten-day stay in West Suburban Hospital in Oak Park, I returned home with casts on each leg from knees to ankles. Kendra and some of her high school friends thought that painting my leg casts in psychedelic colors would aid in my recovery. That was only their opinion, but I let them do it anyway; I was a great brother. I was blessed to have a close high school friend who would come to the house and pick me up for rides around town for lunch, and I could visit other friends from his car. My chores around the house would be limited—no lawn mowing, no work in the garage, and so on. But I did learn to fold laundry, wash dishes, vacuum, and dust furniture from a wheelchair. With the leg casts I was not to stand or walk. Hard to understand for a teenage boy with his own ideas. For some unexplained reason, known only to myself, both casts had to be reinforced part way through the summer.

The next challenge was how to get to high school while wearing two leg casts. We had moved into a new house the year before, in the new subdivision Dad had surveyed with my help. The high school was through a field behind our house, about three-quarters of a mile. The wheelchair could not traverse the field to get me to school safely. We were lucky to have a neighbor in the subdivision that Mom and Dad knew, the assistant superintendent of schools. After my mobility issue was brought to his attention, he had a great idea. The handicapped high school athletic director had recently passed away and, as luck would have it, his three-wheeled golf cart was available. This was a great solution. It wasn't a '60s muscle car, but it would do.

The next hurdle was that I needed to have a driver's license to go on any city streets. So I was off to my next goal. I had to get permission to complete my driver's training course, from a golf cart, and get a driver's license for that particular mode of transportation. Another friend of Mom and Dad's worked for the Illinois Department of Motor Vehicles. He was the instructor in charge of the lo-

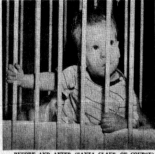

BEFORE AND AFTER (SANTA CLAUS, OF COURSE).
The immediate contrast here will meet the eye at once — the wonder expressed above in the eyes of a one-year-old seeing "Santa" for the first time in his life, and the "faith fulfilled" way in which the small boy at right loves the plush elephant Santa gives him. But the real contrast cannot be seen, for these are children with handicaps that do not show in pictures. The baby behind the crib bars is Dickie Hardine of Galesburg, who entered the hospital with polio last September and is now in Forest Park home–St. Francis division receiving treatment for paralyzed spinal and leg muscles. His first sight of Santa came at the Forest Park home Christmas party last Thursday. At right is seven-year-old Chester, one of nine emotionally disturbed children now living at Abbott Children's Center—first children's mental hospital in the state—on Peoria State hospital grounds. Regardless of the handicaps—physical and mental—these are timeless attitudes of children at Christmas.—Star photo by Ralph Winn.

NOT BARRED FROM CHRISTMAS even though paralyzed spinal and leg muscles keep them confined to a crib, these two post-polio patients at Forest Park home, St. Francis hospital division reach out for the red stockings distributed Thursday afternoon by Santa Claus at the annual children's Christmas party. For Dickie Hardine of Galesburg, admitted to the hospital with polio in September, this will be a "first" Christmas, and Benny Stevens of Creve Coeur, background, is 18 months old. He also was admitted in September suffering from spinal paralysis.—Star photo by Ralph Winn.

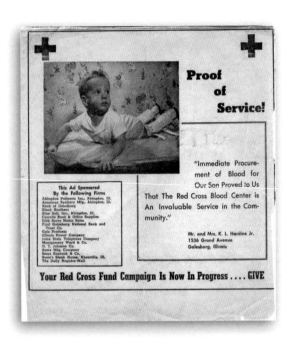

Neighborhood buddies in the '50s

At home in Galesburg, post-surgery

Cub Scout salute with Marc Bullis

Washing the car with my sister, Kendra

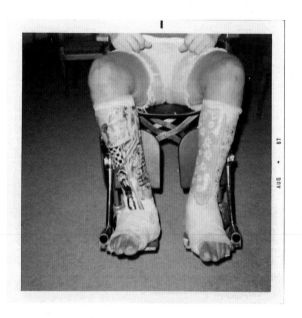

Bilateral leg casts, 1967

Graduation Day

Marrying Karen—October 7, 1978

Our cake

With my parents, Ken and Marge Hardine, on our wedding day

Walking, 1988

At work as an administrator of residential facilities, 1988

Celebrating another birthday with Karen

In our custom-built home

cal licensing office. He came out to the house, gave me the test, and explained the rules, and then mentioned he had never done a golf cart driving test and thought the office would laugh at him. But I passed and the golf cart worked out very well for the balance of time that I was going to have these casts on both legs. When it was raining, Mom graciously gave me a ride to school, on her schedule. As the director of nursing services at the hospital, she wanted to always be at work well before 7:00 a.m., so I got dropped off early and talked to the janitors and roamed empty halls. There were three days that I got caught in a rain shower on the way home in the golf cart. The lack of speed with the golf cart, plaster casts, and rain were not a good mix. Life lesson: carry a garbage bag for a makeshift raincoat to put on the casts.

About three months later, the casts came off and it was time to learn how to walk again. I embarked on a routine of daily exercises that would help maintain the new length of my heel cord and strengthen my legs. This series of exercises was different from the ones in past years. I was to stand close to a wall or kitchen cabinet, keeping my legs straight and leaning forward on my toes to stretch my calf and foot muscles. I got used to my new center of gravity with my feet flat on the floor. After about a month of these exercises, I could feel a big difference in my posture and my ability to walk without falling as much. My self-confidence level increased along with my self-image. I still wasn't totally like the other kids my age, but I felt I was getting really close.

9

OFF TO COLLEGE

"The world worries about disability more than disabled people do."

—Warwick Davis

The summer after my junior year of high school found me back at Lake Lawn Swim and Tennis Club, doing the same duties as the year before. Now that I was getting stronger and more self-assured, I also volunteered for more tasks around the house. I mentioned to Dad and Mom one afternoon that we should put a patio off the back steps. I'd unknowingly volunteered to do it; my male self-confidence kicked in. Dad took me outside to the patio area. We discussed the location and marked off the area. The next morning at about 4:00, before Dad left for work, he explained to me how concrete was to be laid, how thick it should be, how to level it and finish the top, and he left me with a shovel, a tape measure, and a big grin. He then mentioned, as he was leaving, that the concrete would be delivered in three days, along with a wheel barrel. That's what I got for being overly confident in myself! The patio turned out fantastic, with the right elevation, the correct finish, and all the corners square. I wasn't sure I wanted to be involved in construction in the future. It was hard work, but a lot of fun.

Later that year I was elected to be the sports editor of the senior yearbook. I have no idea how or why I was elected, but I took it on and actually enjoyed it. So, in addition to my classes, I was busy my senior year with attending all the sports programs and writing articles for the yearbook. This venture included climbing bleachers, walking football fields, and traversing baseball diamonds. Senior year was surprisingly calm. I was actually able to walk home through the field. It was not the easiest thing to do, but I did it to prove I could. Two girls I had met and talked to at a church social became my friends, and to this day we still stay in touch. Their interest in me was a tremendous boost to my ego.

After graduation I was offered a job at a gas station, working third shift for two dollars an hour. That was big money compared to what I had been making as a lifeguard, a dollar and thirty-five cents an hour. It took a couple of nights on the third shift to get used to working that late, but I thoroughly enjoyed talking to the people who were out all night. It was quite a lesson on how people treat others, how they present themselves, and what their expectations are of people they know versus people they don't. I was happy to be making all the big dollars prior to going to college that fall. I knew college was inevitable. Mom and Dad had made it very clear that when I turned eighteen, I would be on my own. I would be moving out of the house and getting a good education.

I was going to Robert Morris Junior College, in Carthage, Illinois. It had a summer program, but I wasn't interested because I was making so much money at the gas station. About two weeks before the summer session started, though, Mom and Dad came to me and told me that I was going to start school in two weeks. As hard as I tried to argue that I wasn't going until the fall, I lost that argument. They both knew that if I continued to work at the gas station and make that kind of money, I would not want to go to college.

My last weekend at home came faster than I thought. Mom and Dad took me down to the college. I was excited and understood the whole purpose. We unloaded what few items I could take into the dorm room. Then Dad gave me five hundred dollars, said that he and Mom loved me, and told me I was always welcome whenever I wanted to come home. I thought that was kind of funny because I didn't have a car, but there's always a way to figure those things out.

Walking around campus was interesting. It was an old campus—I don't think there was a level surface anywhere, on any of the sidewalks or steps. Luckily, I made it through the two years without falling down. After being on campus for about two weeks I picked up a part-time job at a gas station to help offset the cost of pizza, beer, and other nonessential items. While my mobility was doing very well, my grades were horrible. I was on academic probation and warned that I'd better get back in line. I worked hard to try to get my grades up to an acceptable range, but it was difficult. College was more about new friends and girls for me.

When my two years were up, I moved back home and took a few courses at a local college in the hopes of getting my studying habits organized and grades improved. Dad had me work at one of his asphalt plants, doing load receipts from trucks I weighed and other hot, smelly jobs. I think it was a lesson to get a good education, so I could have a successful career. Dad also bought me a 1956 Ford that needed lots of bodywork. I was suddenly a body-shop expert. No rest that summer.

I then applied to Belleville Area College, in Belleville, Illinois. Luckily, I was accepted into a new program to get an associate's degree in physical therapy. I must admit this program was a great challenge and I excelled in all the classes, ending up with a 3.8 grade average. I was as proud as my parents were. I was equally proud that I had an efficiency apartment of my own. I think I was more successful at Belleville because I was interested in the subject matter of the program, having a connection to physical therapy. It was also easier to study without the distractions of dorm life.

The classwork obviously centered around human anatomy, how and why the human body does what it does and what treatments offer a positive impact of regaining function. One of the classes involved dissecting a human cadaver—not my favorite class but an excellent learning experience. All of my classes gave me a new perspective on polio, my past history, and possible future issues. I came to the realization that my physical ability would always be an issue and that it would slowly get worse. I tried not to think of this, however, and focused on overcoming it.

During the two years at Belleville Area College I kept various jobs to help pay expenses and challenge my physical limitations. The jobs included second shift at a liquor store, third shift at a donut shop, full time on third shift at a nursing home, and Saturdays at an automotive junkyard in East Saint Louis. That taught me a great lesson, learning what people leave in old junk cars: money, drugs, and bodies. We had to call the police when whenever we forced open a trunk and found things like that. Another time, we put a pickup truck in the crusher, not knowing it had belonged to a man who hated the scrap-yard owner. He taped some sticks of dynamite under the frame and the explosion took the crusher out of service for weeks.

Upon finishing my degree, I moved back home and worked as a physical therapy assistant in the Galesburg Cottage Hospital rehabilitation department. I was extremely excited to have this opportunity to apply my education to treating patients. I never thought that I would want to continue on in college, but it so happened that the nurse who delivered me still worked at the hospital as a department head. She would always tease me that she did not drop me hard enough on my head in the delivery room. She was continually very adamant, as was my mom, that I continue to get at least a bachelor's degree or more to further my education and future success.

I applied to Ohio State, Marquette University in Wisconsin, and the University of Alabama. I was accepted at all three, but my choice was Alabama. I wanted to see other parts of the country. My focus was going to be occupational therapy. My strategy was to have an educational background in the physical motor skills of physical therapy along with the fine motor skills of occupational therapy. The University of Alabama—Birmingham campus was huge, way beyond my expectations. The culture of the south was another learning experience. Their customs were quite different from what I was used to, including how they treated women and minorities; how they handled table manners and family life; and even what they ate, including foods like okra, grits, and red-eye gravy.

The one roadblock was that the director of the occupational therapy program felt very strongly that only women should be a part of the program. It was useless to argue with her, so I quit college. I felt let down that I had no support for my journey at that school, but my parents understood my decision.

As if that wasn't enough of a setback, another one was on the horizon. Some friends at the apartment complex where I lived wanted to do a pig roast. I told them I could dig the roasting hole and then cover the pig with rocks and start cooking. Well, by the end of the preparation, a sharp pain in my left foot sent me to the emergency room.

A steel pin that had been put in my foot a few years prior for fusing the bones had started to work its way out. After a shot of Novocain and a small incision, I watched the doctor use a manual hand drill to back the pin out. It felt like a large threaded splinter. There I was, light years away from home, and now what?

10

BEST YEARS

"I want to know you moved and breathed
in the same world as me."

—F. Scott Fitzgerald

Over the course of the next few years, I decided to reinvent myself. I worked a number of jobs, opening my own wood furniture and cabinet shop and selling life insurance in Birmingham, Alabama, and Houston, Texas. While these were worthwhile experiences, they weren't meant to be. I chose to go back home, gather my thoughts, and plan a new direction.

Back home I met with the administrator at Galesburg Cottage Hospital and shared with him that I needed to get a job. He told me if I could create a job, I could have it, an interesting challenge. After some discussion with the nursing and therapy staff I went back to the administrator three days later and shared with him the need for an orthopedic services department. I would assist the orthopedic surgeons and surgery staff with applying traction devices during and after surgeries. He agreed and I was employed by the physical therapy department to apply traction equipment as ordered by the physicians.

The physical therapy department at Cottage Hospital hired an occupational therapist to expand the rehabilitation department programs. Her name was Karen Olson Cheney and she was from Minneapolis, Minnesota. This new hire would change my life in a way I never expected. Thinking back over the years, there were times I'd asked my mother how I would know when I met the right woman. "You will know right away. There will be no questions about it; your heart and eyes will let you know," is the explanation Mom gave me numerous times. Naturally, she was right—she had a knack for that. Life lesson: listen to your mother.

My self-worth increased significantly after meeting Karen. She quickly developed a good understanding of polio, both the history of it as well as future outcomes. Likewise, I was able to get a better understanding of occupational therapy and how it fit into the rehabilitation program. Karen also read me like a book and knew my thoughts. We respected each other, had the same likes and dislikes, and were a perfect match in many ways.

The rehabilitation department formed a bowling team and we were some of the lucky ones to be on it. Karen and I bowled in the league once a week with other teams, starting at 9:00 p.m., and way past my normal bedtime. Tendonitis developed in both of my ankles due in part to how often I walked during the day and, of course, the fact that I was bowling. To solve the problem and strengthen my ankles, doctors prescribed bilateral short leg braces along with custom shoes. The braces helped but made walking difficult and limited my mobility with other activities. I discontinued the braces after a few months and went back to my normal walking routine, minus bowling. My ability to walk and participate in other activities improved tremendously.

Karen and I were married October 7, 1978, in Galesburg, and honeymooned in Vermont. The fall colors of the leaves were fantastic, as was the charm of New England. To this day, our honeymoon is one of our most cherished times. We continue to be happy, and loving and supportive of each other. The year we were married we purchased an old one-room schoolhouse built in the early 1900s out in the country, overlooking a creek. We knew, this was going to be our home. We remodeled the schoolhouse to make it livable and thoroughly enjoyed it. We both did the remodeling tasks and I'm proud to say my physical limitations did not stand in the way of all that work. We had numerous parties at our home, some planned and others on a moment's notice.

Despite this, staying there forever wasn't in the cards. We had taken a few trips to Minnesota and the north woods area of the Boundary Waters. That part of the country looked so beautiful and inviting. We routinely discussed our long-term goal to settle in Minnesota.

My hope was to finish my college education with a master's degree, to make myself more employable. I had been promoted to purchasing agent at Cottage Hospital, responsible for evaluating and purchasing basic medical supplies and equipment. After having a successful year in this position and learning a lot, a hospital near Chicago contacted me with an opportunity at St. Joseph Hospital in Elgin, Illinois. I was to develop a materials management department there and assist three other Chicago-area hospitals, plus one in Santa Barbara, California; all were jointly owned by the Franciscan Sisters. The position involved managing the purchasing department, shipping and receiving all supplies, product evaluation, working with the printing department, and the approval of all capital equipment. This opportunity allowed me to finish my bachelor's degree in applied social behavior and continue on to a master's in management and marketing. I was proud of myself, what I'd accomplished, and also that I wasn't dealing with any late effects of polio, for now.

While I was employed at St. Joseph Hospital, I found myself learning sign language so I could communicate with an employee in the housekeeping department. That department was down the hall from the materials management office. This young man stopped by the office each morning and waved to my staff, and I wanted to learn how he communicated. It was a boost to my self-confidence and made me happy to learn sign language. It's never too late in life to keep learning.

After finishing my master's degree, I had the opportunity to move back to Galesburg and be an administrator for a long-term care company. They had many homes in

Illinois. The newest was an apartment complex of forty units connected to a private pay long-term care facility of ninety beds. They needed someone to open the complex and recruit nursing staff and patients, along with filling the apartments. Of course, I had to get state and federal nursing home licenses and learn the state federal health care rules and regulations.

For about eight years I was involved in the long-term care industry as a licensed administrator. I started up new nursing homes with assisted living complexes, reorganized existing nursing homes, and recruited staff for others. The companies were located in New York, Minnesota, Illinois, and Wisconsin. It was a fabulous experience working with these corporations, as well as the families, employees, and communities with their different goals, cultures, and objectives.

Our married life was busy, traveling to Vermont; Alabama; Williamsburg, Virginia; Alaska; Connecticut; Alberta, Canada; and various weekend destinations. We were blessed to have many great friends with the same outlook on life as us. Karen had found a beautiful lake lot while attending an occupational therapy conference in Alexandria, Minnesota, a wonderful town in the west central part of the state. For her fortieth birthday, I had a log home cabin built on the lake lot. I kept amazing both Karen and myself with my mobility, snowmobiling, operating tractors and an ATV, ice fishing, and hunting. We built out buildings, created large vegetable and flower gardens, split firewood, and got our boats in and out of the water. This was our cabin, but we longed to live there full time.

We moved to our log home in Alexandria, in 1991, after I was offered a nursing home administrator position in Evansville, Minnesota, twenty miles west. We were amazed at how welcomed we felt, like we were instantly a part of the community. I became active in the Chamber of Commerce on their government affairs committee and a task force to develop a snowmobile trail system from the town of Fergus Falls through Alexandria to Sauk Center, approximately one hundred miles. The existing trail system was part of the Otter Tail Railroad system that had not been used for many years. Burlington Northern owned the rights to access on the trail, so it took some meetings and planning to get them on board and permit using it and adding black top for jogging and snowmobiling on the trail. When the trail system was completed, it brought the total length of Douglas County snowmobiling trails to five hundred miles.

I also accepted a position on the board for the Runestone Museum. The purpose of the museum was to display the artifacts, stories, and history of the Norwegian explorers who traveled to Alexandria in 1362 before Columbus landed in America. My other community involvement included joining the Douglas County Public Health board, the advisory board for Douglas County gun range ordinances, and the Calvary Lutheran Church stewardship committee; helping with the Minnesota Concentrated Employment program, Minnesota Lakes Maritime Museum development, and Minnesota Historical Society future planning for Alexandria; and acting as the Ducks

Unlimited Sponsorship Banquet chairman and the zone chairman of the Lions Club International and Rotary Club of Alexandria, Minnesota. Life lesson: when your body isn't slowing you down, keep it busy!

11

REINVENTING THE JOURNEY

"The only disability in life is a bad attitude."
—Scott Hamilton

I had not thought about polio and what I'd been through earlier in life until I fell for the first time in years. I was at a local gas station and being my typical joyful self, walking around and giving the crew a hard time. My left knee gave out and I went right down, causing a torn anterior cruciate ligament in my left leg. I thought perhaps I had broken my leg because the pain was hard to take, especially on the ambulance ride to the emergency room. Surgically, nothing could be done because of scar tissue and my leg muscles relocating from previous surgeries. So, it was time again for a leg brace, to stabilize the knee and what few muscles I had. This incident didn't really bother me because I thought it would be over in a few months. Unfortunately, I was wrong.

The news that the brace would be a long-term solution started me thinking about the late effects of polio: loss of strength, loss of endurance, and increased fatigue to name a few. The troubling part about this fall was confronting my mobility limitations. Things like going to Canada for fishing, enjoying deer hunting, and taking rides in our wooden Chris-Craft boat could be problematic. The most concerning limitation I faced was the difficulty I would have transferring into a car. In addition to these physical issues, the new reality impacted my mental well-being. I asked myself, *How do you plan for and accept post-polio syndrome?*

Post-polio syndrome affects polio patients later in life, with decreasing muscle strength, breathing difficulties, swallowing issues, speaking difficulties, muscle and joint pain, lack of endurance, and inability to get restful sleep. All of these late effects of polio come on gradually, making it difficult for those affected to accept and plan for what is next. Of course, I had refused to accept that post-polio syndrome had come into my life. As walking became more difficult, I started to use a cane as much as I could, but even that wasn't always a solution. There were occasions when I was using the cane on gravel or wet surfaces and the cane would lose its grip and slide out, making me fall to the ground. Standing up after that became an even a bigger hassle and sometimes impossible in snow. My knee brace and weakness in my legs and upper extremities made it a big ordeal to stand back up. It took a while, maybe a year, to master the art of getting up after a fall and I continued to use the cane for support. Life lesson: accept what has been given to you.

For the next eight years, I worked with a rehabilitation company out of Minneapolis, setting up rehabilitation de-

partments in long-term care facilities and clinics throughout west central Minnesota and eastern North Dakota. I
thoroughly enjoyed this journey because the people were
wonderful and the therapists were a pleasure to learn from
and recruit. Thinking back on the success of the rehabilitation departments, I tried to overlook the physical conditions of the residences in the facilities; however, it was
still making an imprint in my memory. The rehabilitation
company was so successful that a company out east ar-
ranged to purchase it. This company asked me if I wanted
to take over marketing and recruiting in a number of Mid-
western states, and while I was impressed with the offer
and proud they'd asked me, I had to decline because of my
health. I realized that the effects of polio would be showing up more in my future, though at the same time, I had
no intent on retiring or even trying to slow down.

A local architect I met at church contacted me one day
to have coffee and talk about project ideas. During our time
together, we discussed what I was planning on doing, if
anything, for work and I was still unsure. He shared with
me that after years of experience and success, he was planning on starting his own architectural firm. Knowing the
skills I had in planning and organizing, he suggested I work
with him on managing construction projects, specifically
nursing homes and small businesses. We also discussed
building custom homes that would be totally accessible to
disabled individuals. After about four more cups of coffee,
we decided that we would work together as separate companies to manage projects and, more importantly, design
and manage the development of universal design homes.

These homes would be created specifically for individuals with a disability or those who may develop a condition that would limit their mobility or access to care in the future. I was also blessed to know a highly respected local interior designer, a close friend who would help on these projects. I developed a client intake form to gather medical information for the designing and building. So much for slowing down and saving my strength and endurance!

Our idea was very successful, and we became the team to design and build for almost any specific illness or disability. We were honored to be one of the first teams to build totally accessible homes in Minnesota. One of our homes was even featured in *Lake and Home* magazine. Our ideas and focus included home designs and construction for the VA system in Minnesota and consulting on designs for the North Dakota VA. I was also called upon in personal injury cases to evaluate remodels for accessibility and to design for new remodels. Life lesson: it's rewarding to use your expertise to help others.

12

HOME AND FRIENDS

*"The language of friendship is
not words but meanings."*

—Henry David Thoreau

In 2001, Karen and I set off to build our own totally accessible home. While living on the lake was beautiful, it was becoming harder to put the boats in the water, till the garden, go snowmobiling and ice fishing, and so on. We sold our log home on Lake Ida as we were starting construction of our new home in the middle of twenty acres of timber.

I decided we needed walking trails so I cut trees and weeds for a one-mile trail system through our property—a lot of hard work but worth it for the beautiful paths. The idea of a small yard to mow went by the wayside with my purchase of a lawn tractor. Of course, there were a number times that I got overconfident with mowing and ran out of gas on the trails farther from the house, or a drive belt broke and stranded me. The worst part of those times was calling a friend to come help me out of the situation I'd put myself in. My friends enjoy telling these stories at dinner parties but change the details, some of which are new to me.

Some of the criteria for the house's layout: no steps into the house from any exterior doors, adequate width of all exterior and interior doors and halls to allow for wheelchair use, wheelchair-accessible bathrooms—one had a large shower with no curb and an accessible sink to roll up in a wheelchair and allow for leg space, and the master bathtub would have a chairlift for transferring from a wheelchair into the tub. We included numerous other applications for the kitchen (cabinet height and toe kick space), garage, pantry, laundry room, and patio. Electrical and mechanical systems were also accessible by wheelchair.

When the house was complete, it was very empowering for me to be able to move around it and not worry about crutches or canes or walkers. When we first built the house, I could still walk with increased difficulty. There were a number of times that I would cry for the happiness of living in this beautiful, accessible home.

I did have a fall on a customer's deck ("Damn acorns!") on a tour with a contractor. I fell to my left and tore my left rotator cuff, but at least it was not my left leg. That fall and my continual use of a cane for walking led me to have ulnar nerve surgery on my left arm.

Another symptom of post-polio syndrome was emotional problems. Obviously, this related to the decrease in mobility, muscle strength, and not knowing when those symptoms would get worse. As I continued on my journey with the custom homes, I realized it was becoming increasingly difficult for me to tour the job sites inside and out and review the progress with builders and home-owners. I also found myself fighting depression and truly accepting the fact that I could not do things that I used to do. Fishing, hunting, snowmobiling, and other outdoor fun-loving activities were now a thing of the past. The depression returns on occasion. The shiny spot is that I am able to socialize with friends and I've realized they don't treat me like I have any disability at all.

I sporadically started to use a manual wheelchair. This was fantastic. I could go outdoors, work in the garage, and transfer to my golf cart with minimal assistance. With twenty acres of timber, a gun range, and a mile of trails, I could not ask for more.

A number of years later, after I tore my rotator cuff, I slipped and broke my right kneecap. Obviously this was considerably worse than the falls I'd had in the past. I recovered slowly but the key word is *recovered*. Not wanting to be disabled and experiencing further falls, I began using the wheelchair more. The accessible home projects continued for a few more years until I had to accept that my mobility, endurance, and muscle strength were continuing to decline. During one of my routine physicals I mentioned that I had some weakness in my right arm. Overuse of a wheelchair and a weak right arm can cause issues in the shoulder and neck muscles. I had an MRI procedure and discovered I needed to have a three-level cervical fusion. This had to be done immediately; if the problem had gotten worse, I could have been paralyzed from the neck down with spinal cord compression.

The cervical fusion was a great success, though sleeping on a reclining chair while recovering from surgery over a four-month period was not the most enjoyable thing to do. With the weakness of my trunk, shoulder, and neck muscles from polio, I was unable to move my body in bed without using my shoulder and neck muscles. It really helped that a close friend made an adjustable book holder for me to use while sitting in a chair or at my desk to minimize excessive neck movement. In spite of having occasional muscle pain, I was glad I had the fusion done and could move on with hobbies and social activities.

By now I was using a wheelchair all the time, and I was unable to stand during a transfer. Using the wheelchair full time did not help me maintain strength or endurance, both of which were decreasing over time. I was able to independently perform a lateral transfer using my arms, however, so Karen and I decided it was time for me to start standing for bone and muscle conditioning. We purchased an electric standing frame. The frame lifts me into a standing position that is secure enough for me to stand for whatever length of time works best. The purpose is to provide compression on my bones from my body weight so that the bones remain strong. Standing upright also assists in joint range of motion and muscle stretching. As always when using assistive equipment that signaled another strength decline, I was hesitant to have the metal frame help me to stand but I quickly got over it. Standing in the frame securely, I could read books, watch television, or listen to music. I have never read so many books in my life!

Breathing was starting to become more difficult, specifically at night. I had been using a CPAP (continuous positive airway pressure) machine during sleep for a number of years to help eliminate sleep apnea. As the muscles of post-polio syndrome patients age, they get weaker. I needed a more sophisticated machine to control my breathing, inhaling and exhaling. I switched to a BiPAP (bilevel positive airway pressure), which controls inhaling and exhaling pressure. It seemed to work. I was now getting a good night's sleep, which helped with reducing fatigue and increasing endurance. With weak throat muscles, I was encouraged to more thoroughly chew my food to avoid choking.

Fatigue is another symptom of post-polio syndrome. 60 to 90 percent of polio patients will suffer from this. It affects one's strength, mood, reactions, and general health as it progresses with age. As I went into my sixties, I continued to fight fatigue with the mindset that I would rest tomorrow. I had the wrong attitude; severely affected polio patients typically need 30 percent more energy to function compared to an average person. I was doing myself more harm than good. Dropping things, having difficulty transferring into and out of the wheelchair, and being afraid of injury when using my woodworking tools became routine problems. Side effects from fatigue are the use of sleeping medications and irritability. Life lesson: accept lifestyle changes.

To help with fatigue, naps became an integral part of my day: midmorning and midafternoon for about thirty minutes. Karen had suggested this routine for many years because I had never taken naps. Again, she was right and I should've started this many years earlier, as it makes all the difference in the world for my endurance and muscle weakness. We also decided it was time to buy a personal hydraulic lift in case I fell on the floor. My first use of the lift would have made a great comedy sketch. In short, your hind end needs to be in the sling, not in the air.

Our next purchase was an electric wheelchair with joystick control so I would not overuse my upper extremity muscles. Then we sold my Cadillac and purchased a handicap van with an automatic lift ramp and a driver's seat that would retract back and turn sideways to accommodate transferring from a wheelchair. As much as I enjoyed driving to see friends, go out to dinner, view the countryside, and shop, I made the choice not to drive anymore. I just did not trust my reflexes or my strength. It's no surprise that Karen did not appreciate the driving tips I started to share with her from the backseat.

I changed my diet and lost about forty pounds by giving up some foods I really loved. The weight loss had a significant effect on my fatigue, blood tests, and joint pain. Another thing I should have done years earlier. It is absolutely amazing how good a person can feel mentally and physically eating the right type of food. My self-confidence and self-image became more positive as well. Through this period in my life, I was amazed and thankful that my friends thought seriously of making their homes accessible so that I would be able to visit and socialize with them. Some of them modified their stairs to a four-inch riser versus a six-inch so that the stairs themselves would be easier to traverse, less height to step up. We purchased a ten-foot wheelchair ramp made of aluminum that folded up for transportation. Not only was this ramp helpful on difficult job sites, but our friends also borrowed it to make their houses easy to access. Thank goodness for true friends; they are so important in our lives. Their support and help has been vital for living an extremely wonderful and blessed life.

All of these changes were extremely hard. But like most affected polio patients, I knew giving in or giving up was not a choice. Living with and accepting post-polio syndrome will continue to be a challenge; nothing can change that. I have a better understanding of dealing with it, which will benefit my mobility, attitude, and safety.

13

CLOSING THOUGHTS

"Go often to the house of thy friend,
for weeds choke the unused path."

—Ralph Waldo Emerson

While writing this book of memories, I found myself on the floor after a failed transfer from my leather chair to my wheelchair. Karen was not home at the time, so I had to wait until she arrived after work to help. This is a difficult point in time for me, unable to be mobile enough to help myself, which will lead to more stories for our friends to elaborate on at parties. Another life lesson: get over it.

There is no indication of how long the progression of post-polio syndrome will take. I don't really know what the future holds for me but I intend to be as mobile, healthy, and independent as possible. Seeing what the years have to offer will be another learning curve, but I am looking forward to it.

I am no longer able to walk. I depend on either the manual or electric wheelchair, and our accessible van, to provide me the freedom of mobility outside the house—going to doctor and dentist appointments, shopping, and gatherings with our friends. I have to be careful not to exceed my own physical strength every day, because overdoing it has a negative impact on my muscle fibers and fatigue. I started taking naps two times a day to help me maintain strength and endurance.

Pacing my activity remains a challenge. I find it difficult to complete projects in my woodworking shop at a quick rate. My hobby of restoring antique guns from the 1800s and antique furniture and appliances is becoming harder because of their size and weight. I participate two times a year, displaying my wood projects, at a wine and art crawl with downtown merchants in Alexandria. The cutting boards, wine-serving trays, and boxes I make from exotic woods are mostly free gifts to friends in the area. My woodworking tools are becoming a safety concern to me. Losing an eye or finger would not help me.

At home, I am currently able help out by: dusting tables, furniture, and floors, as well as cutting vegetables, carving meats, and loading and unloading the dishwasher from my wheelchair. Oh, and sharing my secret experimental recipes while cooking and acknowledging Karen's opinions. I like spices and my Norwegian wife does not. Solution: have spices at the dining room table. With the decreased strength and agility in my arms and hands, using modified utensils affords me a safer grip when cooking, eating, or attempting to follow recipes. When the weather is inclement, I thoroughly enjoy cooking, reading, and watching the deer, turkeys, and birds out our windows.

I can never thank my parents and their friends enough for the plans and tasks they gave me to help with my strength and self-confidence. I also would be remiss if I did not mention my faith in God, family, and our fantastic friends who stepped up to help me, at their choosing, as I progressively became weaker. As I mentioned earlier, several friends made it clear to builders when remodeling homes that they wanted accessibility so we could come by to visit and socialize with them. The contractors whom I worked with on construction projects also always went out of their way to help me access job sites by providing a dedicated parking spot and taking pictures of the inside work for my review, a great help in conserving my energy and endurance. I was even lifted to a second floor by a Bob Cat skid loader for a meeting. After a hospital discharge for a broken kneecap and a long leg brace, a contractor I worked with went to our house, built a ramp by the bed, and lowered the bed height, so I could safely laterally transfer from my wheelchair into the bed. He also went to a close friend's house and installed a grab bar going from the garage into their house. This made it easier for me visit with them in their home.

The local businesses where I purchased my toys—an all-terrain vehicle (ATV), lawn tractor, fishing boat, and golf cart—went out of their way to modify them with hand controls, brake adjustments, steering controls, and seat modifications for easy access and safe trips on our property and trails. The Minnesota Department of Natural

Resources made special hunting permits available, allowing me to hunt from my ATV. Our waste hauler went out of their way over the years to pick up the trash and recycling, traveling down our long, curved gravel drive to our house of about nine hundred feet.

As I have progressed through this journey with polio it continues to amaze me how our friends think nothing of stepping up and offering assistance. I am truly blessed to have such kind friends. It helps me remain as independent as possible and makes my life more rewarding. Socialization with our friends continues to be extremely important and rewarding to Karen and myself. We see it as a key factor to a wonderful, loving life. There is a word that the Danish use, *hygge*, meaning comfortable and cozy. For example, sitting by the fireplace with a warm wood fire, and visiting friends with a glass of wine is hygge.

As I reflect back on the entire journey and think about my parents as well as their loving friends, I am grateful for the jobs they had me do—baling hay, working at an asphalt plant, working as a hospital orderly and mowing yards, to name a few. The lessons I learned of self-confidence, self-image, respect, and self-worth were insurmountable in my successful growth. Our friends were a fantastic team in my success; they were always supportive of my family. The memories I've recalled while writing this book are enormous and uplifting. The journey through all the medical procedures and surgical marvels has been hard to understand and even picture in the entire vision of my life's journey. Reflecting on the different stages and what my parents went through is hard to comprehend. God bless them.

All children, especially disabled children, must be provided with opportunities for their physical, mental, social, and spiritual development. Getting to know your strengths and abilities is vitally important and assists in building self-worth and the ability to understand others. The most important life lesson for me was that although I was not able to be as mobile as I would have liked, this "down time" allowed me to study others, their actions and reactions to events, good and bad. I have been blessed with being able to understand other disabled individuals, as well as people in general. I pray for all children and their parents having a journey similar to mine. I'd tell them to have patience and strength in yourself and others.

People ask me if I would go through this journey again. My answer is always yes. What I learned has made me what I am today.

14

AN OUTSIDE PERSPECTIVE:
COMMENTS FROM FRIENDS

Wife Karen:

When we first met, I bought Richard a suede winter jacket with a fur lining, but he never wore it. Why? The jacket was too heavy for him when he walked. At that time, he was able to walk but was unsteady, and any extra weight was too challenging for his balance. He always avoided walking in crowded areas due to his poor balance and fear of falling if someone bumped into him. As his endurance for walking caused him to be increasingly unsteady, he used a cane for a while but began using a wheelchair in crowded places such as the Minnesota State Fair.

Richard has always been kindhearted and willing to help cook and clean up the kitchen after a meal. He enjoys a clean house and, whether walking or in a wheelchair, has assisted in cleaning by dusting surfaces that were at waist level. He's fed the dog and cats over the years. As he was able, he rode his ATV, or golf cart to take the dog for a run.

One of Richard's traits is to be timely and not late to work, appointments, or social gatherings, which would infringe on others' time. He's often early to appointments or to a friend's house. Parking close to the door is a must so he can avoid excessive walking.

Driving was a given for Richard. He often said he would like to drive me wherever I needed to go, just like his grandfather did for his grandmother (who never drove). Progressive leg weakness, especially following his neck surgery at age sixty-seven, caused him to rethink driving. He had increasing difficulty standing to transfer to the driver's seat. His reaction time was diminishing and it was difficult to lift his left leg to the brake using his left arm, which was the only way he could drive. And why would he use hand controls? We purchased a van with a ramp, and I could then push him up into the van. Yes, he allowed me to drive! On occasion when I was working and he wanted to go to an appointment he agreed to take the transit bus that had a lift for his wheelchair.

Since we were first married, he's wanted the bed covers untucked at the bottom of the bed so he could roll over without getting his legs entangled in the sheets and blankets. He does not have the trunk or leg strength to independently roll over. Richard's had to use his arms to assist in rolling over and I have wondered if also using his neck for this helped contribute to the neck spinal cord compression that caused a spinal cord injury. He had to undergo a cervical spinal fusion. Following the neck fusion, he was forced to sleep in a recliner that automatically moved him down and back up to a seated position. After four weeks I decided to purchase a recliner bed for us. With a bar installed next to his side of the bed, I help him grab the bar and move in the bed to any sitting or lying position he's able. We cannot have heavy bed covers; their weight would prevent movement when rolling over.

For years Richard's weakness prevented him from being able to get up out of a bathtub. He has used an automatic bathtub seat, which allows him to get down in the water and lifts him back up. I kind of like that for myself also. We are not shower people, although we have a fully accessible shower with no step over lip to get in or out.

Now in recent years, Richard's endurance has been so low with resulting fatigue, he has relented to taking naps, something he never did for all these years. The naps help with some of his fatigue but staying up past 7:00 p.m. remains difficult for him. Of course, he does like to get up early, usually by 4:00 or 5:00 a.m.

I am always amazed at Richard's persistence in being independent. He was one to challenge his physical abilities, pushing himself to his limits, whether lifting items too heavy for him, making household repairs, or making many woodworking projects for friends.

Richard has been the most supporting person. He arranges for so many of my interests, having a chicken coop built for me, sharpening my garden tools, snow blowing on his John Deere tractor an area so I could skate when we lived on the lake, or just being there for me. He often makes dinner and does the dishes.

At this point we take one day at a time and cherish each day together. Richard, I love you and always will.

Friends Jim and Anne Eidsvold:

We had the good fortune to be introduced to Richard

in the early 2000s through a home-remodeling project. Jim met him at the Alexandria, Minnesota, Rotary Club and always enjoyed his warm and friendly personality. At this time Richard walked independently with a cane but he never let this slow him down. (Back then, we knew nothing about his life with polio.) He had a confident way about him, was knowledgeable, and had many good contacts that could help us with our project. Our home-remodel project was a very successful journey with Richard's attention to detail, creative thought, and follow-through. There were never any excuses from him because of this challenging handicap in his life. We might even say that because of his polio and his very positive attitude in life, our building project benefitted from his health journey—never giving up!

Our experience with Richard has gone on to become a VERY close friendship. It's certainly a learning experience for us to observe someone who has come to live with the challenges of polio. We have seen a few of his physical highs and lows in fighting the stages of post-polio syndrome but have always observed him rebounding with a positive attitude. We have never seen an individual reinvent himself so many times with respect to his physical capacities as Richard.

Looking back at his career path we see an individual who has taken on multiple challenges, succeeded, and come out on top. He could have let his polio be a negative influence in his life, but he chose to make it a positive. THE POWER OF POSITIVE THINKING IN ACTION!

We have had the opportunity to be acquainted with

Richard's polio journey a little at a time. But now in reading his whole life story we see his perseverance to live a very fulfilling life. We know that all his life, friends have been very important to him, from his childhood to present day. We have been introduced to many fine people through Richard. He always has his group and is the one who organizes them to get together.

You could never find a better, more true, and caring friend than Richard, and we are honored to be his friend!

Friends Bob and Barb Friederichs:

We met Richard and Karen in 1996. The four of us quickly became friends. Both of us have lived and worked with people with disabilities all our lives. When we met Richard he was physically stronger than he is today and we didn't even notice his physical limitations as any sort of impact on our newly found friendship. We did not think of him as someone with a disability, but a survivor of polio. He has always been strong in mind and soul. God gifted Richard with his intellect that has allowed him to adapt to his progressive physical changes post-polio.

Karen has been the most amazing partner in Richard's life. They have utmost respect for each other, and Karen is so devoted to sharing her life with Richard and supporting his safety and independence to the maximum of his physical abilities.

Even though Richard has gradually reduced his physical presence, he has found new ways to support the community and his personal passions of charity. An example of his kindness has been his generosity in helping us support, through his project management expertise, Nordic Meadow Capital Campaign for a major build project. He has spent tiresome hours on this project for gratis, all to support a small community of people with disabilities in Alexandria, Minnesota. The motivation for him was to help this small population of people improve their quality of life.

We have cherished our endearing friendship and life's journey with Richard and Karen. They have been an inspiration to us as a couple, and as well-respected community professionals and members.

Friend Martin Reichel (written March 22, 2020):

Don't look back. Something might be gaining on you.

—Satchel Paige

Ken and Marge Hardine were good friends with my future in-laws, Jack and Marty McFall. Ken and Jack shared the experience of serving their country in World War II in the Pacific Theater and then settled into the community of Galesburg, raising young families like so many other returning veterans. Often, they would get together in each other's homes to celebrate some occasion or just for cocktails, invariably accompanied by cigarettes. Meanwhile, I was dating Jack and Marty's daughter, Jane.

I first met Richard at such a gathering, in the basement of his parents' home. He was wearing dress slacks and a sport coat, so it may have been some special event—or he had been out selling insurance. There was a poster on the wall showing a boy with a smile on his face impishly lifting a woman's dress and peering upward with evident curiosity. I could see we were going to hit it off right away! We had an animated discussion concerning the best places to pick marijuana in the local countryside.

Later he would get married to Karen Olson and buy the old Cook School above Haw Creek in southern Knox County, remaking it into a cozy home. He was, after all, the "Swedish Woodcrafter," a skill that served him well throughout his life, regardless of his actual occupation. I took their wedding pictures in their schoolhouse yard— and together we located a patch of "ditch weed" pot that was promptly named "Maquon Red."

When the commute to their jobs in Galesburg got to be too much, Richard and Karen moved to another quaint house on Prairie Street in Galesburg. It was in the basement of that house that Richard, Reuel Owen, and I built a guitar from scratch on weekends. Richard was always on the lookout for good wood—cheap—and after seeing an ad in the newspaper, Richard and I drove to Rushville, Illinois, to check out a pile of rough-sawn walnut belonging to a guy named Melvin whose last name I don't recall. We loaded his Toyota pickup with as much wood as it could hold. What couldn't be held was Richard's urgent need to pee. So we stopped at a phone booth in Rushville where, under the guise of making a call, he relieved his bladder. After that adventure, my name was changed from Martin to "Mel."

While I had known that Richard was a survivor of a bout with the poliovirus, it wasn't a thing that he dwelt on and for the most part it never impeded him from doing the things we wanted to do. It only became noticeable to me when working in his basement that negotiating the stairs was a bit of a struggle, and so he would stay in the basement until work was concluded and he had to climb them once more. He never complained.

Having gotten into hospital administration at Cottage Hospital in Galesburg, he soon began to move up in the field and it wasn't long before he and Karen, an occupational therapist, moved away for jobs in the Chicago suburbs. Wherever life took them, my wife Jane and I would invariably visit them in their new locations.

Finally, they decided to move to Karen's home state of Minnesota, where they built a log cabin on Lake Ida. Richard led a very active life there, fishing, riding around in his three-wheeler, maintaining and improving his home. He has always been a people person and would befriend neighbors, salesclerks, restaurant waitresses—it didn't matter.

Meanwhile, the after-effects of the virus were gradually taking a toll, so that the long drive to Galesburg, Illinois, became difficult and finally, impossible. Nevertheless, after building a new home that he designed to suit his needs, he made a career out of this talent, working with a local architect, driving around to various job sites as needed. The "Swedish Woodcrafter" was smart, a quick study, and his woodworking skills taught him attention to detail that allowed him to be successful in this new career.

Finally, he was no longer able to drive and so he settled into a well-deserved rest while carrying on his woodworking hobby.

He never told of his trials and tribulations, never complained, kept his sense of humor, and always displayed the warmth that had been a part of his character since I first met him.

As I write these lines, a new, deadly virus is racing around the world, looking for suitable hosts to victimize. Life is a poker game where some get dealt a lousy hand. Richard took the hand he was dealt and played it with courage, grace, and humor. I'm proud to call him my friend.

Friend Betty Ravnik:

I met Richard in 1992. I started the first coffeehouse in Alexandria and although I wasn't in the daily operation of the business, I would begin every day there (before going to the college to teach). Richard Hardine is a very early riser so being at the coffeehouse when it opened was part of his networking and community. It became my community as well. We would chat and, over the months, got to know each other. What I did not know until after I sold the business was that he and other early morning customers came to call themselves the characters of *Cheers*. This group of individuals was very diverse (like the cast of *Cheers*) and I think their glue was Richard. Richard's strength is, and always has been, bringing people together. Community has been family to him.

While owning the coffeehouse I asked our regulars to bring in their baby pictures to create a competition to see who could match the pictures to the person. Richard brought in a picture of himself with his leg braces and of course everyone knew it was Richard. This was a tender moment and one that helped me see part of his journey.

After selling the business we continued our friendship. I had become part of his community. I admired his acceptance of polio. It was not what defined him.

Another phase of our relationship came in sharing our talents in the world of construction. He and I worked on a multitude of new building projects and remodels, residential and commercial. Richard brought to the table a keen sense of project management, keeping people on task while keeping his sense of community family strong.

Through the years I had the opportunity to travel with Richard, our spouses, and friends. During these adventures I witnessed the challenges Richard endured maneuvering travel with a disability. Polio didn't define Richard but it did restrict him. Even with those restrictions, Richard never focused on polio. He worked around it. He has been so good at not focusing on it that it became invisible to those around him. I often would forget he had a disability and I think others did too.

I have now known him for almost thirty years and have watched how polio continues to diminish his physical abilities, but it has never diminished his will and passion for life.

Friend Christophe Lear, Galesburg High School Class of 1968:

I remember the first time I laid eyes on Richard Hardine. Our family moved to Galesburg, Richard's hometown, in the fall of 1963. We moved temporarily to Northland

Subdivision, renting a home for our family of seven, until more suitable quarters could be found. My father worked for Outboard Marine Corporation and had been transferred there from Libertyville, Illinois.

It was warm weather and I was out for a walk down our street when I noticed a group of boys about my age playing basketball on somebody's driveway court. It was a typical scenario, a backboard and hoop mounted onto the garage, just over the widest part of the drive. Being a two-car garage and having a good, smooth concrete drive, it was perfect for a pick-up game of basketball.

As I approached the group, they were physically engrossed in the usual picking and rolling of basketball goings-on, one boy or another tying to shoot, pass, or otherwise outmaneuver the person guarding them. There were lots of elbows flying and pivots being made in order to gain a good position for a shot that, hopefully, would lead to a score. Amid all the pivots, passes, and maneuvers, one boy stood out as the strongest and that was Richard, whom I was introduced to a little later.

As is almost always the case, they were playing "shirts and skins" and Richard's team was skins. It struck me at the time that his upper body was very well developed in comparison to his lower body. He had long legs, but one of the two was less mobile. The problem was that fundamentally, his legs just weren't able to keep up with his stronger upper body in the maneuver he was trying to perform. But that didn't stop Richard one bit. I was amazed at the time (and still am) by how well Richard used the strength of his arms and shoulders to gain advantage and compete in a sport in which most people who'd had polio would ever attempt.

I wasn't as close a friend to Richard as some others, but we often saw each other at teenage house parties and dances. Like most eighth-grade boys, we were interested in the same girls. Later, though, through our mutual love of football, we got to know each other better. It was our good fortune that Richard's home was adjacent to the high school football practice field. Richard had volunteered to be one of our team's managers. On many days after practice his mother was kind enough to allow Richard to invite us over for sodas and snacks. We all had a great time, as only high school boys can have. And everybody wanted to be at Richard's house. We're talking 6'3" tall, 230-pound young men who just finished two hours of football practice, with precious little but water to drink. Richard was amazingly hospitable, but I think his mom played a key role in our mutual fun after practice. As today, Richard was quick with a joke and kept everyone entertained.

Much of my social circle in high school, and eventually in college, was centered around band and choir. Free time, outside of studying and class, usually involved music practice, performances, and any high school musicals, which were offered annually. Richard just wasn't part of that "scene" and we drifted apart until thank God, I met someone who worked with Richard's wife, Karen. My now-wife Sonia is a speech therapist and worked in the same department as Karen. We were all middle-aged by then and before long we had dinner together. As couples we hit it off immediately and we have stayed close ever since. Richard and I could cherish our high school memories, pretty much any time we saw each other.

After only a year or two of enjoying our new friendship, the Hardines moved to Minnesota and we moved to Wisconsin. Even though we are now eight hours apart, we made a pact to meet annually over a long Labor Day weekend each year. Through now thirty years of five-day annual visits, I've had the good fortune of seeing the world through the eyes of my good friend Richard Hardine. I wish I had spent more time with him when I was younger; I missed a great deal, but I am thankful to have the chance to reengage and catch up.

This is all background to the real story, and that is the wonderful, inspiring man Richard is. To truly know Richard, it helps to remember that kid playing basketball. He is nothing if not "determined to succeed." I can't help but think his physical limitations as a child, due to polio, contributed to Richard's character development. We'll never know how Richard would have turned out without the polio. And I'm not wishing such a terrible thing on anyone. But many of the virtues attributable to Richard may well have willed themselves to the surface, as a result of his overcoming the physical challenges of that disease.

One of Richard's most noteworthy virtues is that of self-will. He simply won't be defeated . . . in anything. And a related attribute is his wanting to do the best, at everything. He is a woodworker and turns out the very best at each project. His liquor cabinet is always fully stocked with the best; his humidor has many great cigars and his gun cabinet several noteworthy pieces. But this isn't to brag; many men have the drive to have the best of everything.

For Richard, it isn't a quest to be the best or own the most; it's rather his keen interest in being proficient in the skill *and* knowledge of equipment and their necessary disciplines. He may not own a Sharpe's rifle, but he can carry on an intelligent conversation about them. And this is true of most any discipline. Richard is very funny but also appreciates the humor of others. He is unselfish and one of the best hosts I've ever known. All of these attributes take a self-will that was developed early on in his childhood years. I am a mere sloth by comparison ... thanks, Richard!

Our friend Richard, if he is known for anything, should be known for his extraordinary willpower. Anything at all that he puts his mind to, he accomplishes. He doesn't see the obstacles, only the opportunities. As a boy he developed the will to succeed. And I admire him for it.

Friend Gary Fedo:

I was working as the director of imaging services at North Memorial Medical Center. One day I received a letter from my cousin Bruce's wife in the intradepartmental mail. I thought that was very strange. Why would she send me a letter via my place of employment? As I read the letter, I realized it was not addressed to me but to her dear friend, Karen Hardine. The letter mentioned that I worked at NMMC, and since Richard Hardine had just started working there, we should get to know each other. And so it began.

On my first meeting with Richard, it was obvious that he was a polio survivor and enjoyed doing lots of the same stuff that we did. Soon, Richard became a "member" of a group of guys at North who hung out together. We camped, hunted, and fished together. Richard joined us on numerous fishing adventures. It soon became evident that he was just "one of the guys" despite his polio. Everyone treated Richard just like anyone else.

No one in the group had lots of money so our trips were very frugal, to say the least. We would travel to Canada for fishing but camped out, not at a campsite. We would just pull into shore and pitch some tents. Our only accommodation to Richard was that we would tie a long rope to a tree and extend it down the rocks to the water's edge. This allowed Richard to get up from and down to the boat. That was it. Again, Richard was just one of the guys.

We called the place we camped Camp BUFU. Richard can explain that name to you. Pretty soon Richard had made us a Camp BUFU box for holding all of our cooking utensils. We talked so much about Camp BUFU that my wife almost got me a vanity license plate for my car. Thank God we explained the name before she did. One day it was raining so hard that we couldn't see the boats from camp. We were sitting under a tarp canopy that we had set up in order to cook breakfast. All of a sudden, lightning hit a tree not fifty yards from us. I think all of us thought we had been hit by lightning and were dead—for just a split second.

We eventually got too old for sleeping in tents and rented a home on Oak Island in the northwest angle of Minnesota. Much nicer. No more jokes about bears in camp and how you didn't have to be faster than a bear, just faster than Richard. Unfortunately, no one told the bears. One afternoon, Richard was tired of bouncing around in the boat, so he stayed back at the cabin for the afternoon fishing. He was sitting in the cabin when he spotted a black bear on the deck. He thought that was pretty neat, until he realized there was only a screen door between him and the bear.

Eventually, Richard needed a boat (for no good reason that I could determine, as there was plenty of room in the other boats). Soon he had the "Queen Mary" to my "Blue Goose." He would sit in his boat for hours in his garage, waiting for spring. I will let him tell you about one of the first launches with his new boat (hint: it required a ride in another persons' boat to catch his, as he forgot to attach a rope to it when launching). So, brand new boat. My brother Rod invites us to fish at one of his lakes near Duluth and Richard wants to use his boat instead of my brother's. He might not have done that had we told him the name of the lake beforehand: Boulder Lake. Every time we bumped a rock, a little tear would fall from Richard's eyes. We did catch some nice walleyes, and Richard's boat was officially "broken in."

Richard decided to move to Alexandria and live on a lake. They bought a lot, and he decided to save a few dollars by clearing the trees himself. How the heck was he going to do that? Well, enter his father-in-law and me. We spent a weekend cutting, burning, and pulling stumps (with his baby pickup truck). Two things to take away from this: Richard's father-in-law works harder than the two of us despite being twice our age, and Richard is a bit crazy! We spent an evening cooking steaks on a little BBQ against the corner of the foundation, huddled out of the wind. Did I mention that Richard is crazy? Crazy or not, the work got done and a beautiful lake home was built.

For many years Richard was not treated any different than anyone else in the group despite his limitations. I think that was the greatest thing ever with Richard. Sure, we didn't take him running with us, but we took him pretty much everywhere else.

Unfortunately, we all have aged. Some better than others, but it is harder to do the things that we once found easy to do or we simply can't do them anymore. This has hit Richard harder than the rest of us. It is hard to see his ability to do things disappear, especially since he worked so hard to be able to do things like the rest of us. That said, he has kind of reinvented himself. He's doing small wood-working projects, repairing old guns, etc. He just finds a way to keep on trucking on.

Friend Marden McKee Cullumber:

My friendship with Richard Hardine originated in Galesburg, Illinois, where the two of us were born. Our fathers were boyhood friends and remained so their entire lives despite a military career that led my dad in numerous directions throughout the world. In my growing years, a trip or reassignment for our family was never complete without a stop in Galesburg to see our relatives and visit friends. The times we shared with the Hardines and a third family, the McFalls, were stabilizing influences for me and my sisters, whose lives consisted mostly of change. I remember Richard as a kindhearted little boy who turned into an even kinder gentleman with selfless spirit. Of the seven children in this group, he was the only male. I was aware very early on that Richard had polio though there was never a moment when we regarded him as "disabled" or felt the need to tread lightly around him. Richard was a normal "pesky'" boy despite his illness. He was complete with a full-speed-ahead disposition and the energy to match!

When my father, James McKee, retired from the service in Virginia he and my mother, Ellen, returned to Illinois, where he joined and soon became a partner of a law firm.

In 1979 I was married and teaching in northern Virginia. On a January morning I was summoned to the office of my school, on first period, to find my husband, Larry, standing there. He was notified at work that my father had suffered a heart attack in Illinois. I was needed to assist my mother through the emergency. Larry had already made my plane reservation and was there to take me home to pack.

At that moment how could I know I was about to become reacquainted with Richard Hardine, the compassionate, selfless soul?

I arrived at my parents' home as weather reports warned of a winter storm on Galesburg's doorstep. It was important for me to drop off my bag and head for Cottage Hospital to be by my father's side while my mother remained at home to care for her aging mother.

I was fortunate to be able to speak quietly to Dad a few minutes out of every hour to reassure him that all was well. In between those moments I watched the storm from a nearby window next to the ICU unit. Temperatures dropped and darkness fell. Horizontal wind-driven snow raged throughout the night. It was clear, I wouldn't be shuffling between the hospital and the comforts of my parents' home on Fair Acres Drive any time soon. I was stranded. The town of Galesburg was grounded by treacherous, impassable roads. I was permitted to remain overnight in the ICU waiting room to doze and purchase food in the cafeteria. All I could do to communicate was call my mother on the pay phone and receive local radio reports of the conditions those first few days.

By the end of the second day Dad began to stabilize and there was talk of him being moved from the ICU to a room outside that unit. Mother and Mrs. Hardine must have spoken by phone of my predicament, as word came for me to meet Richard in the downstairs lobby of the hospital the next day. He would drive me home. Eager as I was for a break from the hospital, a major part of me had reservations. I didn't want my dilemma to impose on Richard or place him in danger.

Richard's friendly, familiar face was a breath of fresh air the next day. The roads leading away from the hospital were snow covered but passable. With caution we arrived to Fair Acres Drive, where the next hurdle was immediately apparent: the distance from the street to the door. I'd come prepared for cold weather, but far from equipped to manage weather conditions of this magnitude on foot.

Nevertheless, I said my farewells and thanks to Richard and assured him I could manage from there.

The lengthy walk from the street to the front door was an incline. With blinding white everywhere, it was difficult to gauge the depth of drifted snow so deep I could barely lift my knees and thrust my legs forward. My mother was standing in the open door ahead, encouraging me forward. I was determined with each step to bridge the gap between us. The cold, the wind, the breathing became difficult, and progress very slow. I knew I was in dire straits—so close, but so far away, when strong hands grabbed my shoulders . . . Richard . . . turned me around and led me back down the drive.

Forty-one years have passed since that day. I'll be forever grateful for the support and selfless spirit of my friend Richard, who made a very important decision for me that day, the absence of which could have been very grim.

That he had polio? It's immaterial to those of us who know him.

ACKNOWLEDGMENTS

Karen Hardine, my wife and soul mate, who was supportive and patient while I wrote about my life journey. Memories of events and our love of friends are things we share.

Marge and Ken Hardine, my parents. I am who I am because of them. They taught me love, independence, and to be humble and have respect for others.

Kendra Hardine Brooks, my older sister, who taught me lessons on growing into an adult.

Marc Bullis, my childhood friend, brother-in-law, always there when needed, still to this day, and never let me think I was disabled.

Beaver's Pond Press, including Lily Coyle, owner, gave me encouragement, direction, and support in this book journey.

Special friends spent untold hours supporting me and proofreading the manuscript. They provided fun, learning, respect, socialization, and put up with me.

Surgeons, nurses, hospital staff, and health care facilities have given me a lifetime of excellent professional care, support, honesty, and respect.